ANGEL

ANGEL

HOW TO INVEST IN TECHNOLOGY STARTUPS—
TIMELESS ADVICE FROM AN ANGEL INVESTOR
WHO TURNED $100,000 INTO $100,000,000

Jason Calacanis

WITHDRAWN

HARPER
BUSINESS

An Imprint of HarperCollinsPublishers

This book is designed to provide readers with a general overview of angel investing. It is not designed to be a definitive investment guide or to take the place of advice from a qualified financial planner or other professional. Given the risk involved in investing of almost any kind, there is no guarantee that the investment methods suggested in this book will be profitable. While the method of investment described in this book has been effective for the author, there is no guarantee that the method will be profitable in specific applications, owing to the risk that is involved in investing of almost any kind. Thus, neither the publisher nor the author assume liability for any losses that may be sustained by the use of the method described in this book, and any such liability is hereby expressly disclaimed.

FIRST EDITION

Photograph by Vichy Deal/Shutterstock, Inc.

Library of Congress Cataloging-in-Publication Data has been applied for.

ISBN 978-0-06-256070-4

17 18 19 20 21   LSC   10 9 8 7 6 5 4 3 2 1

To the women who raised, supported, and inspired me: my mother, Cathie, and her mother, Anne; my wife, Jade; and our three daughters, London, Johanna, and Caterina.

and

In loving memory of my friend Dave Goldberg, who was a true angel among men. We miss you, Goldie.

**STOP! DON'T READ THIS BOOK IF YOU
CAN'T HANDLE LOSING YOUR MONEY
INVESTING IN THE RISKIEST ASSET
CLASS ON THE PLANET: STARTUPS.**

CONTENTS

CHAPTER 1

SOMEONE ELSE WAS SUPPOSED TO WRITE THIS BOOK

This book has a singular goal: to teach you how massive wealth is created in the twenty-first century.

It's not a system or a secret, so I'm not going to build this up into something fancy like those bullshit self-help books you've already bought.

I'm just gonna tell you how a C-minus student from Brooklyn (before Brooklyn was cool) clawed his way into the tech industry, got lucky seven times (and counting), and made tens of millions of dollars.

Most folks think I'm lucky, some say I'm a complete fraud, and a handful think I'm a brilliant hype man, and I don't agree with any of them—I agree with all of them.

That's why this will be the greatest business book ever written.

I shouldn't be the one writing it, yet here we are. I'm the outsider who made it in, letting you know how he pulled it off.

I am as shocked as anyone I made it here, and it's a hell of a story: the son of a nurse and bartender watches his family lose everything when the feds—wearing raid jackets just like in the movies—burst in with shotguns to take back his dad's bar. He crosses the bridge to Manhattan with something to prove and, ultimately, he heads to the West Coast to make his fortune.

THE AMERICAN DREAM

The American Dream still exists, it's just not as widely distributed.

Our parents and grandparents took factory and white-collar jobs and rode them for all they were worth in the last century. Now the robots—who never sleep and self-improve on an exponential curve—are taking these jobs. Meanwhile, we humans, with our nagging physiological and emotional needs, struggle to keep up.

Most of you are screwed.

But you're here, so you're clearly willing to learn and I can radically improve your odds if you do the work.

The world is becoming controlled by the few, powerful, and clever people who know how to create those robots, or how to design the software and the tablet on which you're reading this. But please don't stop reading, because I'm going to show you how anyone can get a seat at the table with the digerati, illuminati, and moneyrati and, perhaps, tap into this hundred-year boom.

Yeah, I've got my own formula like those other business

books you've bought, but there is a major difference between my formula and theirs—mine is forward-looking.

All of the other books out there, and some are great, try to explain to you how people made money in real estate, by mastering the art of the deal or by getting the right people on the bus (and the wrong ones off), but they are largely historical documents now.

The world has changed more in the last ten years than it did in the last ten decades.

That's not just some clever one-liner to say in a conference keynote or at a dinner party. It's an undebatable fact.

The changes we've seen with the internet, with mobile phones, with robotics, with sensors, and in biology are mind-blowing not just to civilians, but also to the people working in these fields—and the pace is increasing.

I could give you a list of mind-blowing breakthroughs to prove my point about how fast things are moving, but I'd like this book to stand the test of time, and the truth is that giving you examples like a computer beating a human at chess, or an encyclopedia made with no paid writers, or computers flying airplanes and cars without steering wheels, or wars being won with robots, are so commonplace that science fiction is having a hard time remaining, well, fiction.

I know because the top-tier investors who invested in the last fifty big things call me to find the next big thing. I live on the edge of the future of business and technology.

As an angel investor, it's my job to write the check when no one else believes in you—and that's the most thrilling bet in the world.

Every week I meet a dozen dreamers with insane ideas who want me to give them my money, advice, and access to my Rolodex—but mostly the money.

Oftentimes I'm the "first money" in, the first investor willing to take a chance with a company like Uber or Thumbtack when they are only worth four or five million bucks and almost everyone else has said no.

This year I invested $750,000 in a company that makes a robotic cafe called Cafe X. It eliminates the two most expensive aspects of Starbucks's business: real estate and humans.

When the founders emailed me a video of the prototype in action at a college in Hong Kong, I wrote back to them, "Is this a joke?"

They said, "No, it is not a joke," so I invited them to come to my incubator where we spent three months refining the product and helping them craft their pitch. Then I introduced them to my rich, powerful, and, in many cases, compulsive-gambling, narcissistic friends—who funded the company for millions of dollars.

If we succeed with Cafe X, we will reduce the price of a latte to $2 (again), make it perfectly every time (a computer never forgets how much foam you asked for), and reduce your wait from more than five minutes to under thirty seconds (the machines know where your smartphone is and they make your coffee when you're ninety seconds away).

Instead of a Starbucks on every other corner in a city, there will be a Cafe X machine in the lobby of every building on the block.

Instead of being open fourteen hours a day, these robots will serve us twenty-four hours a day.

Cafe X and other startups will also eliminate millions of jobs in which humans get paid to stand behind a counter and repeat back your seven precious little instructions on how to prepare your morning libation, before pressing one button and masturbating a milk-frothing pitcher for two minutes.

THE FUTURE OF JOBS—AND MAKING MONEY

If right now you think I'm a horrible, marauding, free-market monster, you're only half-right—I'm also a humanist who thinks there are better things for our children to do with their time.

The quicker we eliminate the low-paying, repetitive, and menial jobs, the quicker our species can get to work on bigger issues like sustainability, being multiplanetary, and perhaps retiring the last couple dozen dictators and despots who are murdering, raping, and otherwise oppressing the weakest among us.

Of course, I could be wrong.

When we eliminate all these jobs, the world might spin into a global version of the long-forgotten dry run Occupy Wall Street where a group of savvy but poorly organized hippies and millennials slammed their feet down and said, "No more! We're not leaving until things change!"

Until, of course, the economy rebounded and they got cool jobs with free food and their own private drivers from uber-POOL, then realized that, net-net, things are actually pretty fucking awesome and they don't need to storm Michael

Bloomberg's town house or stink up the Goldman Sachs lobby anymore.

In my mind, candidly, we've got a 70 percent chance of figuring out this massive sea change without starting a full-on revolution in the streets, like we saw in Greece or Egypt, or any other place where unemployment among young adults breaks 20 percent.

But I don't invest in this future because I want to sit in an ivory tower laughing at people whose jobs are replaced. I invest in this future because it's inevitable and I think I can help accelerate the efforts of the founders and innovators who are missionaries, not mercenaries. Of course, I plan to make a great deal of money in these revolutions, but I also plan to look back proudly and know that I helped propel changes that made our planet better.

ESCAPING THE MATRIX

If you're reading this, congratulations! You chose the red pill and you've taken your first step to understanding the bitter truth: the world is going to get flipped on its head two or three more times in your lifetime.

The jobpocalypse is coming, which is not just based on my coffee-making robots. It also includes the elimination of most white-collar jobs we were told were careers, like being a lawyer, doctor, teacher, accountant, pilot, journalist, or—wait for it—a software engineer.

Yes, while the greatest opportunity on the planet today is

probably being a software engineer, I just invested in a company that hopes to eliminate software engineers by letting you type into a box "make me an app that does X, Y, and Z," before spitting out your own version of "Uber for . . . [insert service that sucks right now]."

If you haven't had a panic attack reading this introduction yet, let me tell you the next product I'm looking to back: an artificially intelligent robot that studies humans and builds other robots.

I haven't found it yet, but I probably will by the time you reach the end of this book. The snake is going to eat its tail.

When that happens, there is a good chance that it will be every human for themselves.

By the way, a lot of rich folks have already planned for this outcome by buying islands or huge ranches in remote places like Wyoming or New Zealand (I'm not kidding) that are fully off the grid—complete with solar, water desalination, fortifications, and weapons.

Yeah, there are billionaire preppers, not just hillbilly ones.

A perfect storm of black swans is coming and this book is going to prepare you not only to survive it—but to ride it out on top.

CHAPTER 2

THE BROOKLYN GRINDER

IS ANGEL INVESTING GAMBLING?

Folks in the technology industry debate if angel investing is gambling or actual investing, and it depends largely on how you approach it. Every year I place forty bets hoping to win back more in aggregate than I've put down.

I've invested just under $10 million in the six years I've been angel investing, and the portfolio I've built is worth over $150 million—that's a return of fifteen times my investment.

That's mind-blowing for a kid from Brooklyn who watched his parents fight, at least 90 percent of the time, over money.

More mind-blowing, however, is that the majority of my investment dollars were invested in the past three years ($9 million of the $10 million, in fact).

If you drill down, I invested under $100,000 in the first

year as an angel and hit my two big winners to date, Uber and Thumbtack, in my first five investments.

The return multiple from the first two years of my investing is actually fifteen hundred times.

These startups take ten years to play out, so no one knows exactly where I will sit in the "hall of fame" of angel investing—if one is ever built—but it is safe to say I'll be in the top ten angel investors of all time.

I buy lottery tickets for a living, but unlike the normal schmucks on the street, I get to buy tickets that are in the top 1 percent of the winning pool.

If you have to match seven numbers to win with your lottery tickets, I have to match just two.

I've figured out, and will explain to you in detail, how I've gamed the system. I've rigged the roulette table so it falls on my number ten times more often than yours.

I'm starting every hand of poker with the ace of spades, so my chances of hitting pocket rockets are 1 in 17 while yours are 1 in 220.

If you can't tell already, I'm really excited with where I am in life. Sorry if I sound like an obnoxious narcissist who thinks he's figured it all out—but I actually have. For years people asked me to write books and I kept telling my agent "one more win."

THE SEQUOIA SCOUT PROGRAM'S SECRET ORIGIN

Investing in the cab company that changed the world was that "one more win." When the *Wall Street Journal* did a front-page story on my role as the first "Scout" for Sequoia Capital, the most famous venture capital firm in the world, everything was revealed.

Yep, the brilliant venture capitalists (VCs) who backed Apple, Google, Cisco, Yahoo!, YouTube, Airbnb, WhatsApp, and countless others had started an angel investing program called "Scouts," and I was the first one selected.

Scouts was a simple concept: Sequoia Capital would put up the money and twenty carefully selected founders of technology companies would pick founders they know to back.

The returns would be split: 45 percent to the Scout who made the investment, 50 percent to Sequoia, and 5 percent in a bonus pool to the other Scouts in the program.

This was the deal of the century for us Scouts, because venture capital firms like Sequoia actually only get 20 to 30 percent of the returns when they invest other people's money.

My hunch is that they didn't care what the split was because we were a bunch of nonprofessional investors and the chances of us hitting a home run—let alone a grand slam—were minute. For them, Scouts were a way to increase their visibility into the early-stage market.

The kid from Brooklyn was anointed by the smartest cats in the business. My job was to find the next big thing. It was like George Steinbrenner calling me and saying, "How would you like to help the Yankees win another World Series?"

Holy. Fucking. Shit. YES!

I USED TO DREAM ABOUT THIS LIFE

When I was a kid I always dreamed of having a dad who was a rich banker or billionaire, going to Harvard, and having a trust fund—as opposed to having a dad who almost went to jail.

I'd dream of what it was like to be on the inside and have your college tuition paid for, your apartment in Manhattan gifted to you, and getting $100,000 to invest in a business if you lobbied your parents for fifteen minutes over Thanksgiving—like many of my friends had.

I didn't have that privilege and it put a fire in my belly.

I would sit there on the B train heading home from Fordham at Lincoln Center at ten p.m. on my way home to a three-hundred-dollar-a-month attic apartment on Tenth Avenue, where the only place you could stand upright was about 20 percent of the space in the dead center of the hallway, and think to myself, "What would it be like to be rich?"

What would it be like to have $100,000 on the ATM receipt instead of $100?

What would it be like not to have to worry about money every day of your life? I was so broke that when I was in college I would go to Manhattan at night with two tokens and $2 in my pocket, knowing how to spend it perfectly to get maximum calories from the hot dog vendor by Central Park who charged only $0.50 for a knish instead of $0.75 like everyone else.

I would buy a bagel for $0.50 on the way in, two knishes for lunch, and a third knish on the way home—unless I spent it on a Coca-Cola like an idiot so I could stay awake in class.

When you're broke and see rich people in Manhattan all around you, it makes you curious: "How did these people become rich?"

"PASS ON WHAT YOU HAVE LEARNED."—YODA

So, I studied every system in order to find one that is the most efficient for capital creation, and I believe that it's angel investing in technology. I'm going to tell you everything in the coming chapters because if just one or two hundred of you become angels, it will make an impact on society—plus we can invest together (more on this in chapter 11)!

Heck, if just one person uses this book to back the next great founder who has a world-changing idea, we'll have made an impact together.

There's an outside chance that twenty-five thousand of you might become angel investors, and if that happens, it would change everything.

The world has trillions of dollars sitting in bonds, cash, stocks, and real estate, which is all really "dead money." It sits there and grows slowly and safely, taking no risk and not changing the world at all.

Wouldn't it be more interesting if we put that money to work on crazy experiments like the next Tesla, Google, Uber, Cafe X, or SpaceX?

I'm forty-five years old at the time I'm writing this and I plan on doing five more years of angel investing—I'm on a ten-year plan.

Another two hundred bets and I'm done—then it's your turn.

By the time I'm done with my ten-year plan, I will have invested in 350 startups and my goal is to return $250 million on $25 million deployed—I'm exactly halfway there.

NO GAMBLE, NO FUTURE

Now, gambling has a very negative connotation here in the West, but when I would spend all night playing poker in Los Angeles, with mostly old Asian men, I would frequently hear them say "No gamble, no future," before pushing their chips into the pot, standing up, and rubbing their necks and heads furiously (a tic I soon acquired unconsciously).

It took me a couple of times to understand what these old men were saying, but I quickly started saying it myself, whether I was at the tables or not.

No gamble, no future.

If you learn anything from this book, it's that you must take risks as an angel investor and in life if you want at least the chance of an outsize outcome.

This does not mean you should be reckless; in fact, it means the opposite. I've studied and studied how people have built wealth as angel investors and I've focused on having an unfair advantage over them.

I'm going to reveal every unfair advantage I have developed in the coming chapters so that you can deploy your money intelligently, or perhaps just *more* intelligently than everyone else, which, if you've ever won at poker, you know is the key to success.

If you can't tell who the sucker at the poker table is, it's you, so find another table or figure out how to be better than each of the other players. This might take time, but everything worthwhile in this life takes time and effort.

FOR THE REAL OUTSIDERS

As much as I feel like I'm an outsider—a kid from Brooklyn who didn't go to Stanford and was born into the bottom of the middle class—the truth is I'm a lot closer to an insider than most folks in America, let alone anyone born in the developing world.

Let's face it, I was born a white male in New York City at exactly the right time. I owned a thousand-dollar computer with a four hundred baud modem at the age of thirteen, and I was able to pay my way through night school at a decent college based on the skills I learned using that computer. If I didn't have that computer, I would have ended up becoming a police officer (true story).

Someone living in poverty in small-town America—without that IBM PCjr—certainly wouldn't have had the head start I did. Those facts don't even address the larger, more complex cultural issues around gender and race in our society that I haven't had to face.

I wrote this book to give outsiders a playbook that could level the playing field just a little bit—even if I'm not smart enough to understand or help solve the deeper, more systemic problems myself.

CHAPTER 3

WHAT IS ANGEL INVESTING?

ANGEL INVESTING 101

Angel investing is the act of putting money into the earliest investment rounds of a private business with the goal of getting back more money than you put in—much more than you can return in a safer, more established investment vehicle.

The businesses that angels invest in are typically less than three years old, have little or no "traction," and are trying to find something we call product/market fit. If these businesses didn't look completely crazy, then everyone would want to invest in them and there would be no need for angels. In fact, the term "angel" is used because we are the investors who come to a founder's rescue in their hour of need—when nobody else believes in them.

PRODUCT/MARKET FIT AND EXITS

Product/market fit means that the product the founder has built, whether it's Uber's ride-sharing app or Instagram's photo filters, has found a group that is delighted by it. If a large number of folks find a product delightful, there is a solid—but not guaranteed—chance that the founder can then solve the next biggest challenge: scaling and monetization.

When a founder does figure out how to make money from their product, and they've scaled it to any reasonable level, one of two things happens: the company gets bought by a bigger company or the company goes public.

Those two things are called an "exit" in our world, because that's the time when you cash in your chips—or shares—and get back money (your return).

If a company isn't venture backed, it could just end up a profitable, sustainable business that sends its investors dividend checks. But angels and venture investors hate that. We want exits and returns.

However, most companies I invest in never get past the first milestone of finding product/market fit, let alone figure out how to scale their revenue—and that's okay!

NO RISK, NO REWARD

You're probably thinking right about now, "Why don't you just invest in companies that have product/market fit, have a revenue model, and have scaled to millions of customers?" Well, if a company has hit those milestones, they have probably already gone public!

When you have predictable revenue, you can attract unlimited capital. But when you're just starting out, you can only attract capital from crazy, risk-taking angel investors.

As you add customers and revenue, it becomes easier to value your company. There are several established methods for determining your valuation. But when you're just two people with a prototype, the value of your company is anyone's guess.

For example, Apple and Microsoft in the '80s, and Google and Facebook in the aughts, were all once private companies with very small teams, modest products, and a small number of customers. When they were tiny, they were risky investments and had small valuations.

Famously, Mike Markkula put $250,000 into Apple to become a one-third owner and employee number three. Andy Bechtolsheim, co-founder of Sun Microsystems, invested $100,000 in Google before it was incorporated, and Peter Thiel invested $500,000 in Facebook at a $5 million valuation.

They were the crazy, risk-taking investors who all made the right bet.

"YOU ONLY HAVE TO BE RIGHT ONCE."
—MARK CUBAN

I'm famous for having invested $25,000 in Uber when it was worth around $5 million—it's now worth $70 billion in the private markets. When I invested, Uber was operating in one city and they only had a couple of Lincoln Town Cars signed up.

It wasn't clear if the business could scale or make money, but I knew the founder was exceptionally driven and that I personally loved the product. In my mind, at the very least, Uber was an exceptional product for about 10 percent of the population who already used car services, typically business people in major cities.

That was enough evidence for me to place a bet.

I invited them to an event I hosted, called Open Angel Forum, which was designed to bring together a dozen investors to hear from six startup founders. The night Travis Kalanick presented on a pier in San Francisco at my event, three investors decided to write checks: Cyan Banister, First Round Capital, and me.

A dozen other professional investors passed on Uber and to this day, when I see them, they are reminded of the greatest mistake of their investing careers. Some of my guests invested in the other five companies who pitched us all that night. I don't even remember those companies' names!

Uber will be, almost assuredly, the best investment the three of us ever make. We hit the home run of home runs. Without that one investment, I wouldn't be writing this book.

And that's why angel investing is something that I believe you should consider if you want to create wealth. It can change your life if you suspend fear, squint a little, and focus on not just what could go wrong with a business but what could go right.

While it's unlikely you'll hit a return of five thousand to ten thousand times your investment, like I did, it's very possible—maybe probable if you do all the work—that if you operate for a couple of years, here in Silicon Valley, making fifty or one hundred individual investments, you will return more money than you put in.

Even if you just make back the money you invested in a hundred startups, you will have been able to hang out with the most driven and creative people in the world, building an exceptional personal network, and learning a shit ton.

All while having this amazing lottery-ticket possibility of winning one hundred to ten thousand times your money.

While it's totally crazy to make each of these bets on an individual basis, it's even crazier to not make one hundred of them.

ANGEL INVESTING VS. BORING INVESTING

Now the safest investment vehicles in the world, traditionally, have been things like bonds, treasuries, gold, ETFs (exchange-traded funds), and mutual funds. These devices are highly regulated, safe, and predictable when compared to angel investing.

It's widely accepted that the stock market in the United States has returned, on average, 7 percent a year. It will take you about ten years to double your money at that rate.

Government bonds are trading around their all-time lows at the time of the writing of this book, at 2.4 percent a year. It will take you about thirty years to double your money at that rate.

People are searching for returns everywhere, but returns are becoming harder and harder to find as pools of capital become larger and larger.

I wish I could show you a chart of angel investing, but it's a very opaque practice that can be wildly profitable and the people doing it like it to be opaque. If you found a secret diamond mine that could make you tens of millions of dollars, would you share its location? Probably not.

If you want to double your money every seven to ten years or so, buying some reasonable combination of low-fee index funds is considered the best bet. In fact, a startup I'm a shareholder in, called Wealthfront, allows you to do this with software for only 25 basis points (BPS)—a fraction of what wealth managers typically charge (1 basis point is equal to one hundredth of a percent, or 0.01 percent).

As a bonus, if you use robo-advisors, you don't have to go to lunch meetings with an annoying, superslick money manager two or three times a year—but I kid!

However, you will never, ever, be able to return one hundred or one thousand or ten thousand times your money in these devices.

Angel investing is high risk and high reward.

In fact, it is the highest-risk investing in the world, with much longer odds than playing table games in Vegas, where you have a roughly 5 percent disadvantage at games like blackjack and roulette.

That 5 percent disadvantage doesn't seem like a lot, until you sit at a table for four or five hours, watching your chip stack slowly dwindle away. The casinos know this and they want to give you, at the very least, some entertainment value while they drain your wallet. This is why I've never been able to get comped while in Vegas: I don't play at the tables long enough. Plus I play poker, which is a money loser for casinos.

If you walk up to the roulette table and bet on black or red, you've got slightly less than a fifty-fifty chance of doubling your money thanks to those pesky green numbers that are neither red nor black—they are the house's advantage against the coin flippers.

Why then, if we have very predictable ways to double your money, like index funds and roulette tables, would we ever put our money into unproven startups?

The answer is simple: if a startup in which you are an early enough investor becomes a unicorn—a company valued at $1 billion—you will return life-changing money.

A TYPICAL ANGEL INVESTOR SCENARIO

Let's run the numbers. In the United States, being an "accredited investor" means you are, in the eyes of the Securities and Exchange Commission, smart enough to invest in very risky things like startups.

According to the SEC, an *accredited investor* includes anyone who:

- earned income that exceeded $200,000 (or $300,000 together with a spouse) in each of the prior two years, and reasonably expects the same for the current year, *OR*

- has a net worth over $1 million, either alone or together with a spouse (excluding the value of the person's primary residence).

This next section will walk through how an accredited investor with a net worth of $2.5 million might get into angel investing. If your net worth is much lower than that, don't worry! Later chapters explain how you can leverage smaller amounts of capital to get in the game, and these lessons will still be just as important for your success.

In this scenario, if you had $2.5 million in cash in your bank account and you put it into a fund that returned on average 7 percent a year after taxes and fees, you would double your money every ten years.

If you decided to take 10 percent of your net worth— $250,000—and angel invest it in $5,000 increments, then you have the ability to make fifty investments.

If one of those fifty companies becomes worth $10 billion,

that $5,000 you invested in their angel round when they were worth just $5 million could have a return of a thousand times your investment. That means you would return $5 million.

You would have bought one-tenth of 1 percent of the startup in the angel round and owned one-tenth of 1 percent by the end when it went public or was bought.

However, there is one rub: your shares can be "diluted" over time as the company sells more shares to other investors. The impact of dilution can be mitigated against if you take your "pro rata" in future rounds.

Pro rata means you continue to invest additional money in each subsequent round to maintain your original percentage ownership in a company. It's generally a good idea, but it can get very, very expensive if you hit a major unicorn.

If you didn't take your pro rata in this scenario, my guess is your shares would have been diluted by about 50 percent over time. This means you would own 5 BPS, one-twentieth of 1 percent of this amazing startup worth $10 billion—or $2.5 million.

In the limited and early research done on unicorns—again the $1 billion companies we're looking for—there seem to be a dozen or two unicorns created every year. There are a dozen or so decacorns that have been created in the past decade or so ($10 billion companies or more) including Uber, Xiaomi, Didi Chuxing, Airbnb, Palantir, Snapchat, WeWork, SpaceX, Pinterest, and Dropbox. It seems that every decade or so a $100 billion startup is born. These include: Apple, Cisco, Microsoft, Google, and Facebook.

Now, let's say you hit no unicorns and 70 percent of your investments return zero. I've hit three unicorns in my first fifty investments (two were in my first five investments), but let's say you really suck at this and you hit no unicorns.

You will have burned $5,000 in each of thirty-five of your investments (70 percent of the 50 investments = 35 deals). That's a whopping $175,000 of your invested $250,000 up in smoke. However, it's only 7 percent of your liquid net worth, which we said earlier was $2.5 million.

I think you can live with a 7 percent decline in net worth, can't you? That's not a huge disaster—you won't be out on the street, but you will have taken fifty swings for the fences!

If the last fifteen investments get some return, that 7 percent could be reduced. Here's what I would consider a likely scenario:

Five investments return your capital, so you get $25,000 back.

Seven investments return two times your capital, so you get back say $70,000.

Now you've only lost $140,000, or 5.6 percent of your liquid net worth.

If the final three investments do well, in the way technology investments tend to do, you might see the following:

One investment returns five times your outlay, for $25,000.

One investment returns ten times your outlay, for $50,000.

One investment returns twenty times your outlay, for $100,000.

Now, without any outlandish prediction, you've returned $315,000— you're up $65,000!

So, if you have a net worth of $2.5 million and are thinking about becoming an angel investor, you're basically looking at a likely, worst-case scenario of losing 7 percent, but realistically being somewhere in the range of losing 1 to 3 percent to gaining 20 percent.

To me, that's massive downside protection. It's as if the casino told you that you could multiply your money by a thousand or ten thousand or you could lose 7 percent of your money—how is that possible?!

Of course, you could screw up and return zero—you are investing in highly volatile private companies. If you can't handle losing all your angel investments, I suggest putting this book down now.

WHAT'S THE DOWNSIDE?

Well, you've got to find fifty exceptional companies to invest in, and I invest in only one out of every hundred I look at. That means you need to look at five thousand startups over five years to place your bets—that's twenty startups per week. That's easily twenty to thirty hours of your life every week.

If you want to be in this game, you have to *do the work*.

I will show you how to do the work.

In chapter 11, I'll tell you how to get deal flow, how to find founders to meet with. In chapter 17, I'll tell you what I look for in a founder. And in chapter 18, I'll teach you what you need to ask founders when you meet with them.

CHAPTER 4

IS ANGEL INVESTING FOR YOU?

MONEY, TIME, NETWORK, AND EXPERTISE

In order to be an effective angel investor, you need some combination of money, time, network, and expertise.

You don't have to have all of them, mind you. I've met trust fund kids with no experience, other than being in the lucky sperm club, who jump into angel investing in their twenties by writing a ton of checks at incubator demo days.

I know folks who were broke and busy but had huge networks and tons of knowledge, who weaseled their way onto cap tables by being advisors. In fact, before I had any money, I would trade my network and knowledge of how to promote startups for equity. Twice it actually resulted in checks: sixteen dimes ($16,000) from an advisor position I had with a social network startup that failed its way into an acquihire (*acquired specifically to *hire* its talent*) and 150 dimes from a coupon and deals company that had me on its board.

That's $210,000 from just going to some board meetings, making introductions, and letting founders put my name on their website. Of course, you have to have some type of reputation and industry knowledge to make those kinds of deals work.

There is a long-standing, and totally accepted, tradition of "advisors" getting 10 or 50 BPS—basis points, or hundredths of a percentage point—over two or three years, for helping a startup.

Many times, these advisors call themselves angels even though they don't write checks. Real angel investors make fun of them, calling them "broke angels," but the truth is I've seen many advisors provide more help to founders than their investors did—which makes sense since they got their shares for free!

I'll tell you more about advisors later. Let's see if you have what it takes to be an angel.

DEALING WITH WILD CARDS

The best angels in the world have four qualities, giving them the ability to (1) write a check (money), (2) jam out with the founders over important issues (time), (3) provide meaningful customer and investor introductions (network), and (4) give actionable advice that saves the founders time and money—or keeps them from making mistakes (expertise).

There is another quality that you'll need to ensure you enjoy your time as an angel investor. You should enjoy having coffee with, and talking to, a range of different personalities— including the brilliant and calculating founders who will drive a few of your returns, as well as the delusional and difficult ones, who will be the majority of your returns.

If you're not able to get along with a wide range of people or find it uncomfortable to hear people drone on and on about how they're going to change the world and everyone else just doesn't get it, then this is absolutely not the job for you.

Agents who manage models and actors have to deal with the insecurities of people who constantly need to be the center of attention. Likewise, as an angel investor, you'll have to deal with people who are passionately stubborn and insist that the world change to fit their unique vision.

Some folks call these people visionaries, but that's only after they've made a ton of money and launched products that people can't live without. When you meet them, they'll be just starting out and people will refer to them as assholes, narcissists, and nutjobs.

When someone tells me they have a founder they want to introduce me to but they're worried because the person is a wild card, I set that meeting up for the next day. Angel investors are looking for wild cards, because the best founders are typically inflexible and unmanageable, pursuing their visions at the expense of other people's feelings.

CHAPTER 5

DO YOU NEED TO BE IN SILICON VALLEY TO BE A GREAT ANGEL INVESTOR?

Yes.

CHAPTER 6

WHAT'S SO SPECIAL ABOUT SILICON VALLEY?

SILICON VALLEY IS THE CENTER OF THE UNIVERSE

Over the past five decades, Silicon Valley has emerged as the driving force not only in technology but also in media, transportation, advertising, health, and lodging.

No region in the world drives more societal change right now than the tiny peninsula in Northern California that is made up of cities like Mountain View (a town synonymous with Google and LinkedIn), Palo Alto (Facebook), San Jose (eBay, PayPal, Cisco), Cupertino (Apple), and San Francisco (Twitter, Uber, Airbnb).

If you look at the top five companies in the world by market cap right now, they are all technology companies: Apple,

Google, Microsoft, Facebook, and Amazon. Of those, three are located within fifteen miles of one another in Silicon Valley and the other two are in Seattle.

Of all the venture capital money being invested in the United States, 30 percent is invested in the Bay Area. That's nearly double the money that's invested in Boston, New York, and Los Angeles—combined.

The Bay Area is the center of the world—it's not even up for discussion.

And I'm not just talking about the center of the startup world, I'm talking about the entire world. If you look at how transportation is changing, it's being completely reinvented by Tesla's electric vehicles, Uber's ride-sharing network, and Google's self-driving cars.

If you look at lodging, the most disruptive force is Airbnb.

If you look at politics, Twitter and Facebook are driving the elections—not DC or newspapers.

If you look at advertising, Google and Facebook are making the lion's share of the most important advances with things like targeting and retargeting of consumers. That's a space where newspapers, which have lost 70 percent of their revenue since their peak in 2000, are no longer leading. In fact, more than 50 percent of mobile advertising money is spent with Google and Facebook—and mobile isn't the future anymore. It's everything.

In entertainment, the most important company isn't in Los Angeles. It's Netflix, located in Los Gatos, a town of thirty thousand people formerly known for its orchards. Netflix now has more than eighty million subscribers and is spending more than $1 billion on original content yearly. In just three years,

Netflix has caught up to HBO's level of quality with shows like *House of Cards* and *Orange Is the New Black*. That's even more amazing when you consider that HBO started its Emmy-dominating original programming efforts back in the '90s.

All this from a company that specialized in mailing DVDs to your house in big red envelopes just a decade ago.

LOCATION, LOCATION, LOCATION

Your goal as an angel investor is to put yourself in a position to hit one of these decacorns (unicorns worth over $10 billion) or decade-acorns (the startups that come along once a decade, on average, and become worth over $100 billion).

There are seven tech companies that have topped the $100 billion valuation mark: Apple, Google, Microsoft, Facebook, Amazon, Oracle, and Cisco.

There are dozens more startups that have hit $10 billion, including Airbnb, Uber, Netflix, LinkedIn, Twitter, and Pinterest. At least one of those will go on to be worth more than $100 billion.

So, if you want to succeed in the angel investing world, you're going to do it here, in the world capital of innovation. If the two or three most beautiful and talented models and actors from the drama club at your high school went to Los Angeles to become movies stars, the top three or four developers and entrepreneurs at your college are coming to the Bay Area.

If you're the founder of a company, you can literally pitch dozens of investors every week for half a year here in Silicon

Valley and still have plenty of new investors to meet. If you're in Austin or Los Angeles or New York, you can pitch all of the top investors in a couple of days.

There are dozens of great angel investors in the second-tier cities, but there are more than a thousand in the Valley.

If the best founders are coming here, the best angels need to be here, too.

SECOND PLACE IS FIRST LOSER

If you choose to be an investor in New York or Los Angeles or Seattle, that's fine, but you're going to have to factor in two important things if you want to get a return:

1. You're going to have massively reduced your expectation of having a big win (i.e., a unicorn, decacorn, or a $100 billion–plus company).

2. You're going to have to get on a plane and spend ten days here a month anyway.

If you're going to spend ten days here a month anyway, you might as well just move here and take long vacations in the other place you want to live. You can do this job part-time, but I don't think you can do it if you're based in another city.

In New York, we've seen a small number of billion-dollar exits, including Tumblr (sold for $1.1 billion in 2013 to Yahoo!), Etsy ($3 billion initial public offering [IPO] in 2015), and DoubleClick (sold to Google for $3 billion in 2008).

In Los Angeles, we've seen a small number of hits, including Maker Studios (sold for $500 million to $950 million to Disney in 2014), Oculus VR (acquired by Facebook for $2 billion in 2014), Lynda.com ($1.5 billion to LinkedIn in 2015), Dollar Shave Club (sold for $1 billion to Unilever in 2016), Shopzilla (sold for $525 million to Scripps in 2005), LowerMyBills (sold to Experian for $330 million in 2005), and Snapchat (valued privately at over $20 billion before its IPO).

In other words, you are never going to invest in a decacorn outside of the Bay Area.

LIFE IN THE FAST LANE

Remember that poker analogy I used earlier? Here in the Bay Area, you're starting every hand with an ace of spades—which just makes things so much easier. I've seen plenty of dumb people in the Bay Area get rich quick, and I've seen a lot of smart folks in New York and Los Angeles struggle to break out in angel investing and venture capital.

If you hit a Dollar Shave Club, Lynda.com. or Tumblr in the first round, you're going to be really happy, because you'll get in at a $5 million valuation and exit at 100 or 150 times that— even after your shares are diluted in the later rounds.

Your $25,000 investment could become worth $3 million— which is amazing, but it's still not a thousand or five thousand times your capital. The goal here is to be able to hit a once-in-a-decade company, and those kinds of companies almost always come out of the Bay Area these days.

You can largely forget Europe, with its socialism, red tape, and generally anti-entrepreneurial policies. The one notable exception is Sweden, which has produced recent unicorns like Spotify, King (Candy Crush), Mojang (Minecraft), Skype, and SoundCloud. Some folks argue that it's their focus on design or decreased daylight forcing them to work harder that drives them to win, but for whatever reason, Sweden is on fire right now.

China, India, and Japan are also hot markets for technology startups.

There is only one upside to angel investing in a small market like New York or Los Angeles: you are going to be worshipped. There are so few angels in these regions, you'll be constantly in demand. Also, you're going to feel great about how efficient you are, because there are so few quality deals to review. You'll get your work done early and you'll be all caught up on watching HBO's *Silicon Valley* series. (It's a hilariously accurate look at startup life. They probably get 85 percent right—which is pretty scary.)

NETWORK EFFECT

The term "network effect" means that the value of a network increases with the square of the total number of members or nodes. If a network has ten nodes and you add an eleventh, the network becomes 21 percent more valuable—not 10 percent. It's very powerful math.

We live in a world full of network effects. The nodes in the network here in the Bay Area are the investors (angels, incubators, and venture capitalists), founders, service providers (colleges, lawyers, headhunters, and banks), and the talent pool (developers, designers, and marketers).

The number of folks rooting for and directly helping the startups you invest in will be a thousand times more in the Bay Area than anywhere else. The greatest product Silicon Valley ever built was Silicon Valley—which, generation after generation, reinvests in and propels itself to ever greater levels of efficiency.

In each cycle of technology, the next group of investors and entrepreneurs gets bolder. It was mind-blowing to see Google reach $3 billion in annual revenue in nine years, until Facebook came along and did the exact same thing—in seven years.

Investors in the Valley have learned that when you figure out a money printing machine, like Google's search ads, there is a global market waiting for you to take that machine to. Google now makes 55 percent of its revenue outside the United States.

Facebook watched Google march into dozens of markets and then did it even faster.

Airbnb and Uber watched Google and Facebook expand globally. Then their investors and management teams memorized those playbooks and improved them.

The next group of startups, the ones you'll invest in, will study how these four companies ran the table on dozens of countries, and thousands of cities, and do it that much faster.

Talent is the biggest driver here as rank-and-file developers, designers, and the recruiters who place them hop from rocket ship to startup rocket ship, locking down their four-year stock option plans.

It was very common to see Googlers become "fully vested,"

which means they have earned all their shares, and then negotiate an even bigger package at Facebook, taking all of the lessons of Google's money-printing advertising machine with them. Sheryl Sandberg would be the lead example, having spent seven years at Google before becoming Zuckerberg's number two at Facebook.

Now, you have groups of Facebook executives becoming fully vested, earning all of their shares and watching Facebook's run-up from a valuation of $98 million at their Series A financing to $38 a share at the IPO (a $104 billion valuation) to $128 a share at the writing of this book (a valuation of $368 billion).

With Facebook hitting "escape velocity" and reaching orbit, their employees are now searching all the launchpads for the next rocket ship, valued at $5 million to $50 million, so they can get their slice of juicy, early equity and start the journey anew.

Some of the top executives at Uber and Airbnb include folks who did their time at Facebook or Google.

If you want to make a country album? Go to Nashville.

If you want to make a movie? Go to Hollywood.

If you want to build a startup? You've got to be in the Valley.

LITERAL MOONSHOTS

The cage that tech startups were expected to operate in was ripped open by Elon Musk and Travis Kalanick back in the early aughts when they decided that software, while important, was not going to be the limit of their vision.

Nope, Elon decided to build actual rockets and electric cars—the full stack as we call it—not just the software that kept someone else's rockets on course or someone else's electric cars on the road. In fact, a number of investors tried to pressure Elon into selling just the software and motors for electric cars to legacy car companies like Mercedes and Ford.

After rejecting those suggestions, he launched the Model S, which was rated the greatest car ever by the nonprofit, and highly ethical, *Consumer Reports*. He also broke the safety rating system used by the National Highway Traffic Safety Administration when the Model S was awarded 5.4 out of 5 stars in 2013.

Now Elon is building the batteries that go in his cars and setting up his own mission to Mars. The level of confidence and the boldness of entrepreneurs today is a magnitude bigger than when I started, which is amazing for angel investors. If founders set goals like "colonize Mars," our return on investment is going to be much bigger than if they set goals like "make software for people who want to launch a satellite."

Travis decided to run a marketplace that matched drivers with riders, not just a software system for cab companies like one investor was urging Travis to do. When an investor asked for my support lobbying Uber to be simply an enterprise software company and to stop competing with the cab companies, I replied, "Cab companies are the problem!" and I never discussed the idea again.

Your job as an angel investor is to block out the haters, doubters, and small thinkers, because if you think small you'll be small. I'd rather see my founders fail at a big goal than succeed at a small one.

CHAPTER 7

STARTUP FUNDING ROUNDS EXPLAINED

IS THIS AN ANGEL ROUND OR A SEED ROUND?

When you start angel investing, you're going to hear a lot of terms thrown around to describe the rounds of funding a startup can receive. People ask me about these rounds all the time. "What's the difference between an angel round and a seed round?" "How big is a typical A round these days?"

The funding rounds I'm going describe are not all collected by every startup, and in truth, the majority of startups in the world don't have the backing of angels or venture capitalists: they are called "small businesses."

The following rounds are presented in their natural order, but, again, many founders will skip certain rounds. I've never seen a startup do all of these.

SWEAT EQUITY

The first round of funding in many startups comes from the founders themselves, in the form of working on their business for free for months. It's not an official round of funding. It's the original creation of the business, and, unlike an investment round, the ownership here is paid for with the founders' own sweat. We call this sweat equity, and it should be a useful indicator to you as an angel investor because it shows that the founders are able to create value without capital.

Right now you're probably thinking, "But don't all startups begin with the founders owning 100 percent of the shares?" True. But not all founders are willing to begin working on a startup without an outside investor. Many of them hold out for that first check like it's a security blanket. I prefer founders who are willing to pursue their visions long before an investor comes along and takes some of the pressure off of them.

What this signals, in my experience, is that if these founders someday run out of money—and almost all startups do—they will likely revert back to not paying themselves, while still pushing the company forward with their effort, in order to save the business (and your investment).

These are my people, the hustlers and the builders.

As the world figures out you're an angel, you will be crushed with a legion of founders who want your backing, and most of them will not be the "sweat equity" type.

Most wannabe founders are waiting for an angel to anoint them with a $50,000 check before they start working on anything outside of a PowerPoint deck, or worse, delusionally long emails explaining why everything else out there sucks and their derivative idea will win—if only you believe in them and cut them a check.

If the most a person can create without funding is a Power-Point deck or an insufferable email, they have DQed themselves from running a startup—and you should tell them that in your own style.

I don't recommend using my style, which is uniquely abrasive but works with my personal brand and goals. I typically tell wannabe founders, "I invest in people who build things, not people who talk about building things."

My approach is to be judgmental and combative, if you haven't figured that out. I deploy this style for two reasons: (1) It's who I am; and (2) it is effective in repelling the weak and developing deep, meaningful relationships with the strong.

BOOTSTRAPPING

A variation on sweat equity is called bootstrapping. Bootstrapping means you are using whatever resources you can get your hands on to solve your problem and pull yourself upward, including that little strap on the back of your boots.

A company with sweat equity has built its product or service based on the talents of its team, but a bootstrapped company might have had some outside help—but not from investors. For example, many times the founder of a startup will find a client who is willing to pay for a product that they built with sweat equity.

In that way, a bootstrapped company built off sweat equity is better than a company built on simply sweat equity alone, because it's even *more* resourceful.

When I started my first real business, a magazine called *Silicon Alley Reporter*, it was a bootstrapped company built off my sweat equity. I wrote most of the articles, took the photos, and presold the ads to my friends' companies including Razorfish and the VC firm Flatiron Partners—back in 1995.

Bootstrapping has its origins in nineteenth-century America, when people talked about using the straps on the back of their boots to pull themselves over a fence. I don't want to waste too much time on the origins of words in this book, because when I read other authors do that over and over again, I think, "This prick is just trying to fill pages with information they found on Wikipedia because they don't actually have anything meaningful to say."

FRIENDS AND FAMILY

Startups that have gotten their funding from nonprofessional angels, for example, their rich uncle or friend who made a killing flipping houses, are considered to have completed their "Friends and Family" round.

These folks tend to fall in between the gritty sweat-equity-earning bootstrappers and the entitled snowflakes that won't get started without an angel investor's anointing check.

On one hand, they have the audacity to take money from their families, which if they lose will make for an awkward Thanksgiving, but on the other hand they could be entitled, self-absorbed dreamers who don't mind burning their friends' and family's money.

You can figure out what you're dealing with simply by looking at how efficient and resourceful founders have been who have only raised a friends and family round. For example, if they raised $100,000 from their grandmother and college roommate, and proceeded to give $75,000 of that money to a development shop and $25,000 of it to a public relations firm, well, you're probably dealing with someone who, unlike our sweat-equity folks, doesn't have the ability to build anything.

These kinds of founders are called check writers in my world.

They are often exceptionally good at spending money and spinning yarns, but they frequently become habitual beggars who are so disconnected from the actual product and customers that they don't reach product/market fit with anyone except, wait for it, investors. I'm looking for founders who are scrappy—what we call capital efficient.

SELF-FUNDING

Often, the greatest people you can invest in are the ones who are already investing in themselves. When I meet a founder who says, "I'm currently funding the company," I immediately want to know two things: how and why.

First, how did you get the money to self-fund your startup, and how much have you spent so far? Are you a trust fund kid or did you sell your last startup? Did you go into debt to get to here?

Why haven't you raised money for your startup? Is it because your inheritance is burning a hole in your pocket? Or, are you that serial founder who likes to focus 100 percent on building an MVP (minimal viable product) without having to waste time pitching investors on an idea before you, reasonably, know it's going to work?

When I meet someone who is going into debt to self-fund their startup I get worried—especially if they have a family. In my mind, if you have a family to take care of and you put them at risk to pursue a startup that you can't build with sweat equity, bootstrapping, using your friends' and family's money, or raising money from a professional investor, you are, in all likelihood, insane.

I mean, if you're only investing in your own startup because the hundred other investors—who are more experienced than you and do this for a living—passed on your vision, and you're willing to risk your entire family's future, you're basically saying that everyone in the world is wrong.

That doesn't make you courageous in my book—it makes you either extremely irresponsible or a self-absorbed asshole.

There are many better choices than risking your family's future.

Why not refine your idea? Why not learn to code and invest your own sweat equity in your startup before going into debt? Why not find another startup that has received investments from dozens of angel investors and work with them to change the world? Why not wait until you have an idea that can attract angel investors?

INCUBATOR FUNDING

Founders can also join an incubator or accelerator in order to get a modest amount of funding. Most incubators will give founders $25,000 to $150,000 in seed funding for 5 to 10 percent of their startup.

There are incubators focused on health care, hardware, enterprise software, mobile, and various regions of the world. Incubators have only become popular in the past decade in Silicon Valley and are, in fact, partially responsible for the explosion in the number of startups we've seen.

The other important reason the number of startups—or startup experiments, as I like to call them—has increased so dramatically is that the cost of getting a product to market has dropped from millions of dollars to, typically, anywhere from under $25,000 to $250,000.

Most great companies did not come out of incubators (Uber, Facebook, Tesla, Google), but once in a while a great one does. In fact, there is only one $10 billion–plus company to ever come out of an incubator, and that's Airbnb. Zenefits, Stripe, and Dropbox, valued in the single-digit billions, also came out of incubators. We will talk more about incubators in chapter 23.

Some startups have now started incubator hopping, jumping from one program to another, collecting $100,000 and a bunch of advice as they do, but with the compounding cost of repeatedly diluting their cap table.

If a founder is faced with shutting their company down or giving it another shot at a second or third incubator, I don't think that's a bad thing—it's certainly better than shutting down.

SEED/ANGEL FUNDING

Most founders get their seed round by successfully completing two or three of the five early-stage funding strategies above. For example, someone might bootstrap their way to an incubator by having presold their software to two companies before getting their angel round.

Essentially, your job as an angel is to monitor people coming out of these channels and pick out the best ones.

You're basically acting like a college scout watching high school players, who are still developing, run up and down the field. You can't pick perfectly, but you can develop strategies to pick well.

That's what this book is really about, helping you pick better.

Some notable founders, delightful products, and hot markets can command a seed round out of the gate—skipping the five stages above. For example, if you made a seriously beautiful app in the on-demand space in 2014 or 2015, when Uber and Airbnb were red-hot, you might quickly find yourself raising a $1.5 million seed round before launching.

We often see founders who sold a startup to Google or Facebook quickly raise a significant seed round after simply building a basic prototype or, even crazier, just a slide deck.

Investors can get very excited when a category or a founder breaks out, and when they do, they lower their standards because they believe the wind will be at the startup's back. This makes some sense. If someone built and sold a company to Google or Facebook, their chances of doing it again—or going public this time—are greatly increased, because they've been to the rodeo before.

BRIDGE ROUND, A.K.A. SEED PLUS

Most founders underestimate the amount of time, and consequently money, it will take to reach the milestones they need to raise their next round of funding. When a seed stage startup runs out of money before having reached the targets that would make a VC firm fund a Series A, or before hitting breakeven or profitability, they do what's called a bridge round. It's called a bridge round because it's a bridge between where they are now and where they need to go.

This round of funding typically comes from the same investors who did the seed round. Those investors are faced with losing their investment if they don't continue to fund the startup, so they tend to be motivated to "close the bridge."

Participating in a bridge round can lead to putting "bad money after good," where an angel funds a struggling startup, or even one that is now likely to fail, out of loyalty to the founder or out of their own ego—but not based on the core fundamentals of the startup.

I've done this many times, because I'm an optimist and I want to believe, and in my earlier days as an angel investor because of ego. If a startup I invested in failed, then I must have been wrong. And I hate being wrong.

These days, I look at each bridge round I'm asked to participate in with a simple question: What has changed since I made my original investment?

If the thing that changed is my faith in the founder's ability to execute, or that we learned the market truly doesn't want or need this product, well, it's a fairly easy response to the founder: "I'm going to stand pat" or "I'm not going to participate in this round."

Founders will often want to know why, and I'm inclined to be candid with them, but I don't necessarily suggest you do the same. Most other angels I see will simply say, "We are not investing right now" or "We don't do follow-on funding," even though they really mean "We only do follow-on funding for breakout successes and founders we really believe in."

Oftentimes, the answer to "What's changed?" is that the founder and their team have learned a ton about their customers, they've built a promising product, and they've learned what they need to do in order to hit breakeven.

In those cases, it's fairly easy to justify a continued investment.

There is one serious caveat to all of this: the valuation and terms of the bridge.

If the seed round was at a $4 million valuation and the company has learned a ton and landed some customers, but the valuation has stayed the same, you should put more money in than you already have. It's a better deal. The company is more valuable now.

If the seed round was at $4 million and the company is asking for the bridge to be at $8 million, you should simply ask the founder, "How did you arrive at that valuation?" I like to leave a long pause after that question, so the founder can speak their truth and I can understand if the shares are, in fact, worth twice as much.

If they aren't, I can simply say, "I'm going to pass based on valuation."

Sometimes a founder will have raised their seed round at $8 million and accomplished a decent amount, but no one will fund their bridge at the same valuation. In this case, an investor or founder can suggest doing a "down round" or a "pot sweetener."

A down round simply means you're going to change the value of the company, making the people who invested in the last round mark their investment down. When the market crashes, like it did in 2000, 2001, and 2008, many startups went through down rounds.

Another way to deal with a bridge that won't close is to keep the valuation the same but give the bridge investors a "pot sweetener"—a bonus. There are a couple of financial and legal devices to do this. One is a liquidation preference. Another option is issuing warrants.

In both cases, the investors will typically get two or three times the value of their cash in extra stock. So, if I bought 10,000 shares at $8 each, I might get another option—a warrant—to buy 10,000 shares for $0.01 each in the future.

Here in Silicon Valley people like to have "clean terms," which means they shy away from devices like warrants and liquidation preferences. In fact, these are currently considered predatory by most professionals in the Valley.

Now, on the East Coast or in Europe, where investors are much more conservative and have had much less breakout success than in the Valley, they tend to deploy these "downside protections" often.

SERIES A

The Series A is the most coveted and important round for a startup because it is typically done by a professional venture capital firm that will join the board and create proper "governance."

Proper governance means there is a board of directors that holds board meetings that have board resolutions that are all designed to increase the share price of the company.

Before the Series A, founders typically answer to no one. There is no board, there are no board meetings, there are no board resolutions, and no one is focused on the stock price, because the focus is, quite correctly, on trying to find product/market fit.

Once you have a Series A, the chief executive officer (CEO) is going to spend about 20 percent of their time "managing their board." This means, setting up a board meeting every six to ten weeks, or six to eight times a year. They will prepare a board deck, have a lawyer create resolutions around stock options for employees, and they will essentially have a boss.

As an angel investor, you will sometimes have an opportunity to invest in a Series A, but not often. Why? Because VCs are greedy and have huge stacks of chips. When they figure out that a startup deserves $5 million or $10 million in funding and a $12 million to $25 million valuation, they are going to slurp up every share they can find. In fact, sometimes the "lead investor" on a Series A will have the right to approve the other investors!

If you're getting into a Series A alongside a powerful VC, you either have a great relationship with the founders, who are demanding you get an allocation, or you provide massive value and the VC thinks that you owning shares in *their* company will increase everyone's share value.

If one of *your* startups, that you've angel invested in, gets a Series A from a known venture capital firm, you want to plow your chips into the pot and take your "pro rata" as much as you can.

Pro rata means you get to keep your percentage ownership in a company. Typically when you angel invest, you don't get pro rata rights—unless you demand them, and then you do. I won't do a deal without pro rata rights anymore. If someone doesn't think I deserve to get to keep my percentage ownership, even though I was one of their earliest supporters, well, I'm not the right investor for them—and they're not the right founder for me.

It's disrespectful not to give angels pro rata rights. Period.

SERIES B, C, D, E, F, AND MEZZANINE ROUNDS

After the Series A, you're probably no longer actively investing in the company, and it's well on its way to an exit. In fact, if your angel investment is starting to raise a Series B, C, D, or further rounds of financing, it's probably time for you to consider selling some part of your stake in what's called a "secondary" stock sale.

Remember the old adage, when they asked the rich man how he got so rich: "By selling too early."

We'll talk about exits in chapter 30.

But first, we need to get you into the game.

And I've got a hack to help you get started.

CHAPTER 8

HOW TO BE AN ANGEL INVESTOR WITH LITTLE OR NO MONEY

CAP TABLE BASICS

As an angel investor, your job is to provide a combination of money, time, network, and expertise to startups in order to "get on the cap table."

The cap table, short for capitalization table, is the official list of all the shareholders in a company and it includes how much they paid for their shares and what class of shares they each own. Different share classes have different benefits. We'll talk about the differences among share classes and ways to protect your angel shares in chapter 30.

The easiest way to get on the cap table is to simply buy shares, but this requires two things:

I. Money

2. Access to the deal

When you start meeting with startups to angel invest in, you will mostly be meeting with founders who have been unable to raise funding for their startup. The best founders, like Mark Pincus (Zynga) and Evan Williams (Blogger, Twitter, and Medium), for example, are able not only to pick from the top angel investors—thanks to their exceptional track records and networks—but also to fund their companies themselves from their past exits.

Those founders don't need you, they don't need your money, and they are not going to meet with you. You need to find founders who will become the next Mark Pincus and Evan Williams.

The only way you'll get into a hot deal early on is if you are invited into one or you get lucky. When you first start investing, you should meet with as many people as possible but invest in as few deals as possible.

Basically, you should go on a lot of dates, but don't propose to anyone yet. We still need to cover building your deal flow and talk about how to behave before, during, and after pitch meetings.

FIVE WAYS TO GET ON A CAP TABLE

In simple terms, there are five kinds of people on a cap table: founders, employees, advisors, angels, and VCs.

Companies don't exist without founders. They start out owning 100 percent of the company. Over the life of a company, it's the founder who will do the most work. Every minute of a founder's life—awake or asleep—is spent working on their startup.

Employees will spend the second most amount of time working on a startup, but their existence isn't 100 percent tied up in the business. Unlike founders, employees usually get their equity from an option pool. An option is the right to buy a certain number of shares in the future at a much lower "strike price" that was based on the company's valuation when the option was awarded. Options are a great way to align employee motivations because now they are part owners in the business, too. Options typically vest over four years. So, if an employee leaves the company after only two years, they only get to keep half of the options that were granted and the rest go back into the pool for future employees.

Third is the advisor, a.k.a. the broke angel. They trade their skills, time, connections, and reputation in exchange for shares.

Fourth is the angel investor. That's you! Your entire life is not consumed by a single startup. Your job is to support founders when no one else will and steer them into the hands of professional investors.

Fifth is the venture capitalist, a.k.a. the VC. They come in later on, once a lot of the risk has been removed, and their job is to help the company in its transition from adolescence to adulthood.

SHAREHOLDER MOTIVATIONS

Each of these five kinds of owners is working toward a common goal: increasing the value of the business—or at least they should be.

In fact, that's why shares in a company exist. They're a score-card that allows everyone to easily understand what's at stake.

If you're an angel in a startup with fifty million shares issued and an enterprise value of $5 million, then every share is worth ten cents.

In this scenario, if you owned 2 percent of the company you would have one million of those shares. Two co-founders might have fifteen million shares each, their employees might all be participating in a five million share option pool, and a venture capital firm might own ten million shares (20 percent of the company).

You can now all make decisions based on trying to get the company to a $50 million valuation, which would, with fifty million shares outstanding (accounted for), reflect a $1 a share price—a tenfold increase from the seed round when the company was valued at $5 million.

When faced with decisions, such as "Should we sell the company for fifty million dollars?" or "Should we raise ten million dollars for twenty percent of the company?," you can have a candid discussion—informed by the cap table.

In fact, this is a very common situation that shareholders face: Should we sell the company now or raise more money and sell later?

For the two founders, with fifteen million shares each, they will often be tempted to sell their company early. In this scenario, they would be faced with a $15 million payday each, which is hard to turn down when you probably have massive credit card and student loan debt, a modest startup salary, and zero savings.

For the angel who paid $100,000 of their own money for their one million shares, getting back $1 million would be a fantastic and compelling outcome—$900,000 in profit! They also might consider selling half their shares to investors in a new round ($500,000 worth) as "idiot insurance" in case the company eventually fails, while letting the other half ride.

In that "sell half" scenario, they've returned their $100,000 investment and taken down $400,000 in profit on the investment, while still having 1 percent of the company's shares riding on future growth. If the company fails, they will feel like a genius because, well, they made five times their investment while other shareholders lost everything.

However, if the startup becomes a unicorn worth $20 a share, they are going to always think about the 500,000 shares they sold for $1, leaving $19 per share in growth—or $9.5 million—on the table. Of course, when they sell the other 500,000 in shares for $10 million, they will have returned $10.4 million on a $100,000 investment—or 104-times return—vs. $19.9 million in cash—a 199-times return.

This is a great problem to have. Once more, as the old saying goes, "You get rich by selling too early."

The point being, there are only two numbers that matter: how much you put in and how much you got out. How much your shares were worth at their peak is not remotely as important as when you choose to sell them. Many Facebook investors sold their shares shortly after the IPO at $18 a share, when Zuckerberg couldn't figure out mobile. Those investors missed the run-up to $130 a share when Zuck did master mobile, fueled by his seemingly insane, unilateral decisions to acquire

Instagram ($1 billion for a startup with thirteen employees at the time) and WhatsApp (for $20 billion or so).

OTHER PEOPLE'S MONEY

When you look at the venture capitalist on the cap table in our $5 million startup, you have to understand they are operating on a much different formula because they are investing OPM—other people's money.

VCs invest OPM and get a 20 percent "carry," or, simply put, 20 percent of the gains. In our example, if the VCs who invested in the startup owned ten million shares, for which they paid ten cents each, they would have a cost basis of $1 million for the investment. If it appreciated tenfold, to $1 a share, they would have a gain of $9 million, of which the VCs—the decision makers for those shares—would get 20 percent. That's $1.8 million, a great payday, except most VC firms have six partners chopping up that gain, each getting $300,000.

In other words, the angel would have a $900,000 gain, but the VC on this deal who has five other partners is only getting $300,000—one-sixth of 20 percent of the $1.8 million gain. That's only one-third of what the angel, who put their own money to work, would get.

What do you think that VC is going to suggest when faced with a $50 million exit that earns them enough money to pay for, probably, ten months of family living expenses in Silicon Valley? They are going to say, "Let's keep going. Let's build a unicorn!"

The VCs also have a board seat, in all likelihood, and would push hard to get the founders to swing for the fences—and rightfully so. If the company becomes worth twenty times more, that individual VC is going to pull down twenty times as much in carry—$6 million for each partner!

Startup founders often sell too early, leaving money on the table. VCs often force founders to hold out and swing for the fences, risking blowing up companies and locking in gains. We angel investors are generally along for the ride. The good news is that our industry has figured out this divergence of interest and has come up with an effective way to address it: secondary share transactions.

If a founder with 35 percent ownership in their company has no money in their bank account, and they get a $100 million offer for the company, they are faced with a $35 million payday— life changing to be sure. Now, in today's modern age, I think the first $5 million you make is "take the edge off" money. You now have a decade of capital to rest on. However, when you break $10 million you have "escape velocity," where you will never have to work again. The $500,000 in yearly interest you net should cover your life for a lifetime.

However, when you get over $20 million, you're in the "fuck you money" zone, where you can tell anyone to go fuck themselves. It's a dangerous test of a founder's resolve in my experience to go from being under the gun to being able to tell anyone who stands in your way to go make you a ham sandwich.

SECONDARY SALES

This is where secondary sales come in. What a VC firm will do is offer to buy some of the founder's shares to provide the "idiot insurance" we talked about before. This is a delicate balance, and it usually results in a founder being able to sell 10 to 20 percent of their position, which in this case would be $3.5 million to $7 million, which after taxes would be somewhere in the "take the edge off" money range. This is the preferred amount of money VCs like to give to a founder to give them the freedom to keep going because it doesn't distract them. It simply allows them to buy a fancy car, fly business class, get a decent house, and pay off their student loans.

VCs really don't like to have founders get to "escape velocity" or "fuck you money," because it could result in them coming in to a board meeting and saying, "Fuck you, I'll fund the company," or worse yet, "calling in rich" saying, "I don't need to deal with your bullshit anymore. I'm going kitesurfing on Necker Island for the rest of the year."

For angels, secondary shares are a wise way to "dollar cost average" your returns. If you have a chance to sell 25 percent of your position once or twice before the IPO, it would be wise to do so because we've all seen companies worth billions go to zero many, many, many times.

The velocity at which startups can rise in technology is second only to how quickly they can implode. Remember, these are rocket ships and sometimes they blow up right before they reach orbit—just ask Elon Musk!

BROKE ANGELS

But what if you don't have money? Is there a way to get on the cap table? As we discussed in chapter 4, there is a group of folks known as advisors who trade some combination of their networks and knowledge—and sometimes freelance work—in exchange for shares in a company.

Advising startups is often a great stepping-stone to becoming an angel. I will tell you all about my ups and downs as an advisor in the next chapter. I'll even name names.

FOUNDING VS. FUNDING

Additionally, there are two more ways to get on the cap table: you can found/co-found a company or go to work at a company and vest shares over time. Of course, if you do those things you are going to limit yourself to one lottery ticket (or cap table) every four years (the amount of time required for folks to "vest" their shares as a founder or employee at a company).

In twenty years as a founder or early employee of a startup, doing absurdly hard and underpaid work, you will have taken three or four swings at bat. Since 70 percent of startups fail, my guess is you will have one, maybe two wins in your career. However, there is a significant chance that you will have no exits. The chances of missing a 30 percent chance at a win three times in a row is roughly 3 percent (30 percent * 30 percent * 30 percent = 2.7 percent). Also, there is a chance that a "win" could be minor, which is to say, you make only $1 million or $2 million.

The likely scenario, in fact, is that you spend twenty years of your life busting your ass and probably have a decent win and make a couple of million bucks. It's not a bad outcome, but it's not an outsize outcome like we're shooting for here.

As an angel investor, I invest in thirty startups a year—one every other week or so.

Being a founder is amazing because you get to build what you want to see in the world and you're the "god-king/queen" at your company, but the odds are wildly against founders making a huge return, while the odds are in favor of a lifelong angel or venture capitalist getting rich.

Of course, to be an angel or VC, you need to have those chips, skills, network, or knowledge to put to work.

CHAPTER 9

THE PROS AND CONS OF ADVISING

As I mentioned in chapter 8, there are five types of people on the cap table of a startup: founders, employees, advisors, angels, and VCs.

Founders and employees earn their shares by working full-time on building the company. They come to the office every day and vest their shares over four years, and all of their eggs are in one basket.

Angels and VCs buy their shares in a company, they don't go to the company's office every day, and they split their attention between many different companies—and finding new ones.

Advisors to a company don't pay for their shares with cash but rather by providing their resources to the company, be they skills, Rolodex, or reputation. They add their personal brand equity to a startup's often nonexistent brand equity.

YOU'VE GOTTA START SOMEWHERE

Early in my career, I didn't have the money to reach the minimum investment required by most startups, which is typically $25,000 or $50,000, but I did have a Rolodex, connections, and a lot of startup skills—especially in marketing and public relations.

So, I joined the boards of advisors and boards of directors at a number of startups in the hopes of getting some cash.

I became an advisor to a handful of startups including Wealthfront.

I joined the boards of ThisNext, Savings.com, and Dyn.com.

I advised a total of six startups, with the typical commitment being two years of service. Of these seven deals, shockingly, three resulted in me making about $700,000. One of them, Wealthfront, is still very much in play. Only a couple of them actually shut down. Disappointingly, one startup's founder, influenced by a douchebag venture capitalist, screwed me out of advisor shares I had earned. I'll tell you that story later in this chapter.

My guess is Wealthfront will be as big of a return as Dyn, putting my advisor/board record at two home runs, a double, a single, and two strikeouts. That's an absurd .667 batting average and probably not very replicable or sustainable.

OPPORTUNITY COSTS

These days I only take a board seat in my portfolio companies if—and this is a major condition—they are surging or under some sort of unfriendly attack that requires me to join the board to protect them and other shareholders.

Outside of my own investments, the only way I would join a board of a startup is if the founders were friends or I were massively passionate about the company. Why? Life is short and the return of being on board these days would be de minimis compared to my returns as an investor. Of course, it's great to pick up another hundred or five hundred dimes as a fee for serving on the board, but considering those paydays require fifty to two hundred hours of meetings and work over two or three years, there is a serious opportunity cost to them.

Opportunity cost is an extremely important concept in life, so let's talk about it here for a moment. My definition of opportunity cost is "the lost gains resulting from the misapplication of your time."

For example, if you were a startup chief executive officer and decided to spend twenty hours a week for ten weeks teaching yourself design in order to save yourself $10,000 hiring a freelance designer, that might seem like a great way of advancing your startup while you keep your costs low—but how would you know for sure?

It's simple to calculate. Just ask yourself what else could you have done with those two hundred hours and what impact it would have had on your startup.

In this case, the founder could have cold emailed a personal note and sent a follow-up email to three hundred angels (twenty minutes for each, six thousand minutes total) and met with the top fifty of them (two hours of time each with travel, for a total of one hundred hours). If you landed 1 to 2 percent of the three hundred emails you sent, that would be three to six new angels. Those angels would typically invest $25,000 to $100,000 each, for somewhere between $100,000 and $250,000 total invested in your startup.

Now, compare the outcomes of those two efforts: saving $10,000 or raising $100,000 or more—which is a better use of your time? Clearly the latter, which means there is a huge "opportunity cost" for our non-designer founder to wasting their time learning to design.

Unless, of course, this startup in question does not have the ability to raise money yet because the design sucks and the founder has no track record. In that case, we would be comparing the ability to raise zero dollars after emailing three hundred angels with the ability to get your product "investor ready." Those ineffective emails trying to get meaningless meetings would be a huge opportunity cost vs. making a sexy product off of your sweat equity (see chapter 7).

How to allocate your finite time and energy efficiently is something you constantly have to revisit as an investor, founder, parent, and human being. The cost of not revisiting your allocation of time is great, leading to massive regret at having spent too much time on a startup, marriage, friendship, or investment that is destined to disappoint you or destroy your soul.

As you read or listen to this book, you need only look around you at the countless people on the subway or bus or freeway who are thinking about the opportunity cost of their lives.

I can't tell you how many times, as I've struggled to write this book, I've asked, "Is this the best use of my time?" What if no one reads this book that I've spent months writing—and will spend many months promoting? What else could I have done with the hundreds of hours I've put into these tens of thousands of words?

You can pay me back for sharing all these secrets, collected over years and written over six months, by taking these techniques and delivering massive returns. If just one of you becomes a billionaire, centimillionaire, or decamillionaire because of this book, it would please me to no end. When you do, invite me on your private yacht and let's eat some expensive surf and turf and toast to the fact that you were too scared or oblivious to allocate your time correctly until you read my words.

I'm counting the days until someone emails me and tells me this book changed their lives—and the lives of their friends and families—forever. It's gonna happen, I'm sure of it. I wonder if it will be you, yeah you, right there smirking as you read this, who will have the brass ones (balls or ovaries) to cut the check in the next Google, Facebook, Apple, or Uber.

MY FIRST ADVISOR CHECK

Back in 2004, I was broke and trying to get something going. My first startup, a print magazine called *Silicon Alley Reporter*, had been sold in a fire sale to Dow Jones. I was effectively paid two years of salary for seven years of effort. I had moved to Santa Monica to be with the woman I would eventually marry and I was treading water.

My friend Mark Jeffrey, who had let me crash on his couch when I was coming up in the industry, introduced me to his partner Jas Dhillon when they started a business social network called ZeroDegrees. I found out about the service in early 2003, half a year before LinkedIn launched and three years before Facebook was available outside of colleges. ZeroDegrees was even featured on LinkedIn's competitive landscape slide in their now-legendary Series B pitch deck.

I was a simple advisor to the company. I met Jas every couple of months for breakfast at the Ritz-Carlton in Marina Del Rey to give him product feedback on this new category of startup.

When the company was sold to Barry Diller's IAC (Inter-ActiveCorp) in 2004, I got a handwritten check for $16,000. It was a magic moment for me, getting rewarded like that when someone else's hard work paid off, and it made me want to participate in even more startups.

SAVING UP

A couple of years later, after I had sold my blog company to AOL, I was getting a lot of attention from the press and the investment community because I had mastered the art of building a startup by using content, search engine marketing (SEM), and search engine optimization (SEO).

A company called Savings.com, which had a small office a mile from my $2,200-a-month two-bedroom apartment in Santa Monica, asked me to join their board of directors to share my knowledge.

The board had a bunch of venture capitalists on it, and it became clear to me that these boring meetings were becoming much more fun, hopeful, and entrepreneurial because of my presence. I was starting to become known not only as a marketing guru but also as a motivator of CEOs.

In this case, the company got sold to a larger competitor and I got paid $150,000 for my service on the board—over ten times what I made at ZeroDegrees for being an advisor.

I was moving up in the world.

DYN-O-MITE!

On April 21, 2012, I got an email from Kyle York, who worked at a startup almost no one in Silicon Valley ever heard of in New Hampshire called Dyn. They were looking to raise their first round of funding and wanted an independent board member who would help them navigate raising money and the profile of the startup, so I guess they asked themselves, "Who's got the biggest mouth in Silicon Valley?" and decided that was me.

In their email, they explained that they had reached millions of dollars in not only revenue but also profit. I was shocked and delighted to get this email because being able to get on a rocket ship before it takes off is always a good idea, and Dyn was already in orbit when they asked me to get on—which is extremely rare.

"Yes, I would like to be transported to your rocket ship that is already in orbit," I told them, and for two years, I worked in much the same way I did at Savings.com, bringing excitement, hope, and marketing strategies to the company and board meetings. My podcast, blog, emails, and conference had made me into a microcelebrity in Silicon Valley—as did my investment in the "cab company"—and I put my full effort into promoting Dyn, calling it "the Google of the Northeast," a label that stuck.

A year after I finished my two years of service to the board I executed my stock options, which were going to expire. It cost me tens of thousands of dollars to do so, but my faith was instantly rewarded when, three months after I did, the company was bought for over $600 million by Oracle.

My payday was almost a half million, more than thirty times what I made as an advisor to ZeroDegrees and triple what I made as a board member at Savings.com, all without having to be an investor in the company.

Being a board member or advisor is nice work if you can get it, but you have to be willing to put the work in over a decade in the tiny startups that need you before the bigger companies that don't need you as much will let you join their boards.

Even today, with a much higher-profile reputation, I've yet to be asked to join a major public or pre-public board like Twitter, Snapchat, or Google. This is understandable since I haven't done it before, but still frustrating for me since it's on my professional bucket list and I see so many dopey people join these boards and drive companies like Yahoo! into the ground.

Perhaps if one of my investments goes public, I will get that opportunity to join a major board, but for now I continue to grind it out one investment at a time.

COLLISION COURSE

On a trip to Chicago to speak at a conference about mobile startups, I was contacted by a local entrepreneur who had been reaching out to me for a couple of months to get involved in his startup in the gift card space.

Let's call him "Alex."

Like me, Alex was a Greek and he was passionate about his startup, so I agreed to have lunch with him. Candidly, it was easy to choose between sitting with a bunch of mobile advertising tech executives in bad suits eating dry hotel ballroom chicken or going for local Greek food with a passionate founder.

The kid was dialed up to 11, he had major plans to take over the world, and, although his business had a horrible name and was kind of unsexy, I thought there was something there. I had a rule about investing in startups outside of Silicon Valley (see chapter 5), but he didn't need money at the time, so I accepted his offer to be an advisor.

For a year or two, we did regular calls. I introduced him to the top venture capitalists in the Valley and generally did what great advisors do—whatever is asked of them by the founder.

Alex was a hustler and the son of a very successful grocery store scion. His Instagram was a nonstop feed of private planes and popping bottles not only at famous clubs but in the booth with his arms around the DJ.

Alex was a player.

The future looked bright for the business, but it had a long, clunky name. I told him over and over that he needed to have a more polished brand if he was going to make it in the big leagues.

He called me one day with some amazing news. He had acquired a five-letter domain name.

Let's call it "Money.com."

I was over the moon. Even though we were just buying and selling gift cards right now, in the future a name like Money .com could help us expand into other categories without having to rebrand—just like Amazon doesn't need to come up with new brand when they launch new products like Kindle, Fire, Web Services, Echo, or Alexa. They just put those words after "Amazon."

At some point, he bragged to me that he got Jay Z to become an advisor just like me. He even sent me Shawn Carter's signature page. I was blown away because I know Jay Z takes his brand seriously. How in the world did Alex get Jay Z interested in a site that resells gift cards? I was so impressed by Alex's hustle—I couldn't knock it.

Years later he bragged to me that Jay Z didn't execute his advisor shares paperwork by the deadline, so he canceled them. I was perplexed because it's really bad form to talk someone high-profile into being an advisor and then drop them on a technicality.

It would be like asking Steven Spielberg to put his name as an executive producer on your TV show as a favor and then cutting him out of the deal when the show became a hit. You just don't do it. It's petty and it's small and it's dumb because all you have in this life is your reputation.

I found out that a new venture capitalist was "cleaning up the bad deals Alex had done" and I realized that if they were willing to throw Jay Z under the bus, they would have no problem throwing Jay C under the bus as well.

I fought with the new venture capitalist a bit. After all, my paperwork was signed. I didn't miss any deadlines. But it turned into an argument over whether I'd lived up to my end of the deal and delivered the value they expected. Finally, they demanded that I land a couple of employees for the company—like literally recruit and hire developers for them—to keep the shares I had already earned.

That was never what I had agreed to do.

In the end, my Greek brother Alex didn't even have the courage to tell me the news directly. He had his chief financial officer cancel all of my shares. He didn't even give me a token tenth of my shares, let alone the 75 percent of them I had vested and earned.

I could have fought him on it, but the truth is, I've done so well in this life that fighting with a founder just isn't worth it. I'm sure that's what Alex and his investor were counting on.

I considered leaving this story out of the book, but since I've only been screwed by a founder like this once, I thought this was an important story to share. Also, I'm still fond of Alex, I believe in the business, and I wish him well. Maybe when he reads this he will reach out to me and buy me some saganaki and we can settle up like grown-ups over Greek coffee.

I'm still fairly certain Alex will be a great CEO someday. If you're willing to screw the greatest hip-hop artist of all time and an early advisor who you doggedly pursued, you're probably gonna make a lot of money—at the cost of fans and friends.

The point of this story is to remind you that advisor shares are not guaranteed, and in the private company game, there are very few rules and very many ways to screw over your partners. You only have to look at Mark Zuckerberg's early lawsuits—and settlements—to see how ugly and often these things go down.

You're going to need to have a great lawyer, have clearly defined deals, and be selective about the people you partner with. Even when you do all of those things, you're still gonna have people try to screw you. It's the nature of money, power, and, most of all, shares in companies.

People can get really ugly when they see how many shares everyone else has on the cap table.

THREE OUT OF FOUR AIN'T BAD

Looking back on my experiences with the founders of Dyn, Wealthfront, and Savings.com, each has been thrilled to have me as an advisor, they have continued to engage me over the years, and none have begrudged me the value that my shares had accrued or tried to renegotiate our deal after the fact.

In fact, the founders of Savings.com and Dyn were proud that their success got me a big payday. We won together and we are set up to do more in the future.

Having good and bad experiences as an angel or advisor helps you improve your ability to pick great founders—and avoid the bad, immature, or clueless ones.

Life is short, you should spend your time working with the good people, and if you do get screwed, look at it as a small price to pay for getting that person out of your life.

CHAPTER 10

GOING STRAIGHT FROM COLLEGE TO ANGEL INVESTING

THE SUCKER AT THE TABLE

If I could go back and do it all over again, I would have graduated college and gone directly into angel investing. When I was in my twenties, I was sharp as a tack and knew that certain companies, from Microsoft to Cisco, were going to be huge.

Having spent years "playing computer," as my parents used to call it, I knew the entire ecosystem and it was obvious to me that Windows was a massive step function from DOS for Microsoft. The command line interface, with its obscure language, made computers a secret club, but the graphical user interface and mouse made it McDonald's. If I had bet on Microsoft back in the 1980s, when I witnessed this change, by getting my father to take $1,000 from a hot Saturday night at his bar or my mom to do five double shifts as a nurse, my family would have had a fortune twenty years later.

Heck, if I had made a $1,000 bet on Microsoft in 1984, two years before it went public, and when I got the first PCjr computer—running DOS and a Microsoft Basic Cartridge—we would probably be millionaires.

Why didn't I take that chance? I had the insider information from my sixty hours a week "playing computer," but because we thought poor, we stayed poor.

There is no reason anyone reading this right now couldn't figure out a way to scrape together $500 or $1,000 to start placing bets. The average American spends over $100 on their cable bill every month and you can make $18 an hour driving for a ride-sharing service. If you simply quit watching cable TV for five years and took the five hours a day that the average American spends watching TV in that time and used half of it for driving and half for searching for deals, you would have over $15,000 to apply toward angel investing—a year.

At $2,500 per company, that's four bets a year—twenty bets over five years—during your self-imposed boob-tube ban. What if you got a hundred times your return on one? What if you got a thousand times your return on one?

Yum! Yum!

However, most of you reading this have been trained by society, your parents, and your friends to be helpless, so you spend your free time lying on the couch, watching TV, sliding into depression—instead of actively placing bets on your future.

You've been hoodwinked. Bamboozled. Fooled. Slipped the mickey.

Fallen for it.

You're the sucker at the table who doesn't realize that you're just another monthly subscription, and random ad clicker, for corporate America.

It's time for you to unplug from the Matrix and realize that you don't need to pretend you're rich by getting the premium channel package, and actually get rich by taking intelligent risks.

THE FUTURE IS ALL AROUND US

At my second real job, at Amnesty International, I installed their first computer network. Instead of the dozen senior executives in the company using a dial-up modem to get their email on a 2400 baud modem attached to a dedicated phone line in their office, we were putting Ethernet cards into everyone's computers and running Ethernet cables through the walls and having all the computers on a LAN (local area network).

It was clear to me that Novell, Hewlett-Packard, Cisco, and countless other vendors in this era were going to print money, but yet again I missed the boat. If I had taken just forty hours of my pay—at an amazing $10 an hour—and invested it in Cisco in 1990 when they went public, I would have bought about 10,000 shares. Thirty-seven years later, those shares would be worth $300,000—and that's the growth rate of a public company. Private companies can grow much faster.

If I could do it all over again, I would have put "Computer

Specialist & Angel Investor" on my business card, asking everyone I knew to introduce me to hot startups. I would then beg the founders to let me invest in exchange for consulting around IT (information technology) issues—trading my knowledge and meager cash for equity.

Even if the investments had failed, even if people had laughed at me calling myself an angel, even though I was only investing $500 at a time, I would have learned a heck of a lot and met a ton of entrepreneurial people.

You can make your own luck in this life by putting yourself next to the people who are already winning.

CHAPTER 11

HOW TO HACK ANGEL INVESTING: SYNDICATES

THE EASIEST WAY TO BECOME AN ANGEL

To be a successful angel investor, you need to invest in dozens of companies and do it in the hottest market in the world: Silicon Valley.

However, when you're starting out as an angel investor, you're going to suck at meetings and picking companies because, well, you're so new at this.

What if you could invest in ten startups in the next thirty days, but instead of having to pick them yourself, you could simply invest alongside other angels who have been doing this for many more years than you. Might that interest you?

What if you could do this all from your laptop and for as little as $1,000 per investment. Might that interest you?

This was impossible to do ten years ago, but over the past five years, a handful of platforms have emerged that allow angels to syndicate deals via a legal construct called a special purpose vehicle (SPV).

ANGEL SYNDICATES

There are a number of sites offering angel syndicates here in the United States including AngelList, SeedInvest, and Funders Club.

At these sites, successful angel investors create an investment group, or syndicate, where they explain what they typically invest in, what they've already invested in (their track record), how much they typically invest per deal (typically $10,000 to $100,000), and how much in "carry" they will charge you on a successful exit.

Carry is short for "carried interest," and it's defined as the share of profits that go to the fund manager—in this case called the syndicate lead.

The term dates back to the sixteenth century, according to the Wikipedia entry, where captains of ships would charge merchants 20 percent of the profits from cargo that they took the risk and effort to "carry" around the world.

On these platforms, the syndicate leads typically take a 15 percent carry and the platform itself takes another 5 percent, for a total of a 20 percent carry. This is exactly how venture capital firms charge their own investors, who are called limited partners (LPs), with one critical difference: fees.

Venture capitalists typically charge what's called "20 and

2" to their LPs: 20 percent carry and a 2 percent management fee. The management fee is money advanced by the LPs to the partners in the venture fund in order to pay for their overhead (salaries, office space, tickets to expensive conferences like TED and Davos). Those management fees get paid back out of the returns, but they are a point of contention with LPs in the venture capital industry. On a $300 million fund, a 2 percent management fee is $6 million per year. For a seven-year fund, that's $42 million in management fees! Many LPs think these fees are extreme and want them reduced.

With angel syndicates, you simply pay the carry. There are no fees other than some minor legal and filing fees (typically less than $10,000 per deal, spread out across the dozens of investors in a deal).

Individual angels like you can sign up for a syndicate (like mine) and make a nonbinding pledge to invest a small dollar amount per deal. On my syndicate, the minimum is $1,000, but most syndicates set this number at $2,500 to weed out the more casual investors.

When a syndicate lead shares a deal, each of the syndicate members gets a chance to evaluate the deal via an online profile for that startup that typically includes a pitch deck and why the syndicate lead is investing.

A syndicate normally negotiates an allocation with the founder of the startup, typically $200,000 to $500,000 (or 10 to 50 percent of a seed round). If the syndicate can pull together enough investment interest, the deal is consummated.

If the syndicate lead invested $20,000 in a deal personally, while syndicating another $200,000, they now represent $220,000 in this round of funding.

So why do people do this?

Founders love syndicates because they can leverage an established angel investor to round up dozens of smaller investors for them.

Founders also love angel syndicates because they exist as only one entity on their cap table: the SPV. This means they don't have to collect dozens of investor signatures when doing future deals. Instead, they just need to get one signature from the syndicate lead who legally represents all of the other investors in the group.

Angel syndicates love the program because it can easily triple their returns, simply by sharing their deal flow. In the example below, if I invested $20,000 in a startup and got a 20 percent carry on $300,000 raised from a syndicate, and the company had a ten-times return, the leader of the angel syndicate would get a return of $740,000 vs. $200,000 on their $20,000 investment.

How? It's simple. I would get back ten times my $20,000 investment for $200,000, as well as a 20 percent carry on the $2.7 million gain from the syndicate's return—for an additional $540,000!

Now, syndicate members love syndicates because they can invest in startups that more established angels have (hopefully) vetted. It is possible you can invest alongside a lazy angel who doesn't do a lot of thinking before they invest, but even in that case you would have had, at the very least, the ability to make bets alongside someone with some sort of track record. Plus you don't have to say yes to every deal. You can always opt out.

The only thing you give up by being in a syndicate is 20 percent of the return, which seems like a fair trade of services. At the time of this writing, platforms for doing angel syndicates were still very new. The jury is out on exactly what the levels of returns will be, but the fact remains that they are an efficient and low-risk way to get some experience in angel investing.

In fact, I was the first syndicate on AngelList and in two years I did fifty deals—the most any individual had ever done—with more than $12 million invested. I'm a huge fan of these platforms because they give angels the ability to work as a group toward a common goal: increasing their portfolio companies' value and chances of success.

If syndicates had existed twenty years ago, I could have started angel investing when I was only twenty-five or thirty years old, because back then I wouldn't have put $1 million to work angel investing. I could have just put $25,000 to $50,000 of my own money to work.

This is the great angel investing hack that syndicates provide. Whether you put $1,000 or $100,000 into a startup, you're still an angel in that startup, reaping all the cachet that comes from that association. You can meet with founders before and after you invest and build deep relationships with them by asking the right questions, which also allows you to provide material help to those founders on their journeys.

That's why I advocate that new angels do ten small angel syndicates before they start doing direct investing. Beyond the very real chance of getting a positive return on your investment, if you do this hack, you will build your reputation, have a chance to prove your worth to founders, and jump-start your network— all for the bargain price of $25,000. That's only 20 percent of the cost of an MBA and you can do it in a month!

THE BENEFITS OF SYNDICATES

As a neophyte angel, the benefits of starting your education and investing adventure with syndicates is huge. You can, if you choose to, do all of your investments in your underwear or while working at your current job. (I don't recommend doing both of those things concurrently.)

Syndicates require very little paperwork and you can choose to invest without taking any meetings or doing any due diligence. The only thing you need be able to do is prove that you're an accredited investor here in the United States and have your wire transfer clear.

After you make ten investments for $2,500 each, you'll be on the cap table of ten startups along with dozens of other investors. After just one month and ten deals, you will have a network of hundreds of co-investors, as well as a network of twenty to thirty founders you have invested in, since most startups have two to four founders these days.

Once you have ten investments, you can list them all on your LinkedIn profile, in your Twitter and Facebook bios, and on your gorgeous-looking, $15-a-month Squarespace website. (I missed investing in Squarespace—damn it!)

You'll also be able to be as unapologetic and gauche as I was in my early career and put "Angel investor in . . ." in your really long email signature.

Once you have the phrase "angel investor" on your online profiles, you will have instant deal flow.

It will be an ugly and desperate deal flow at the start, since no one knows you and how brilliant you are, but it will be *your* deal flow—and that means something because everyone in this industry starts as an outsider.

Unless your last name is Draper or Conway, you weren't born into this business. Some of the biggest outcomes in our industry have come from people without track records like Larry and Sergey at Google and Zuckerberg at Facebook.

There is a chance that the founder of the next big thing might stumble upon your profile while searching LinkedIn or browsing AngelList and—boom!—you might be the person who takes a meeting with them and gives them their first check.

Someone has to write these early checks. Why not you?

CHAPTER 12

MONTH ONE: YOUR FIRST TEN SYNDICATE DEALS

PICKING THE SYNDICATE DEALS TO JOIN

As we discussed in the previous chapter, investing in angel syndicates is a wildly effective hack as you start your angel investing journey. Every month, dozens of startups are syndicated on AngelList, SeedInvest, and Funders Club.

As an angel investor, you are going to need to invest in fifty startups (diversification!) in Silicon Valley (location!) over three years in order to have a chance at an outsize return. That's one to two startups a month.

You should plan to put $1.5 million to work in these fifty deals, which is $30,000 per startup on average. However, you're probably going to want to put $1 million into the first forty-five deals and an extra $100,000 into each of your top five winners. This gives you a chance to get a five-times return on the winners, any one of which might go to a fifteen-times return based on the inside knowledge you have—and return your entire $1.5 million invested.

In the investment community, we have a term for an investment that returns all your capital invested: a "dragon." So your job is to find dragon eggs.

Right now, however, we want to get your résumé filled with ten quality angel investments that include dozens of well-known, successful angels.

When you visit the various sites offering syndicates and browse the deals, I suggest looking for these basic characteristics:

1. A syndicate lead who has been investing for at least five years and has at least one notable, unicorn investment

2. A startup that is based in Silicon Valley

3. A startup that has at least two founders (with two, you have a backup in case one quits)

4. A startup that has a product or service that is already in the market (you're not qualified to invest in startups that haven't released their products—and frankly you don't need to take this risk)

5. A startup that has either (a) six months of continuous user growth or (b) six months of revenue

6. A startup that has notable investors

7. A startup that, post-funding, will have eighteen months of

cash remaining, commonly referred to as runway (ask the founder and syndicate lead how many months of runway they will have post-funding)

If you invest $2,500 in each of these ten startups, you will have invested at the end of this process $25,000. If your goal was to invest $1.5 million in fifty startups over three years, you've just gotten the first ten under your belt for less than 2 percent of your total chip stack.

Note: "Chip stack" in this book refers to the amount of money you've allocated to your angel investing. Chip stack in poker refers to the chips you have on the table during a single session and is only a portion of your bankroll. Your bankroll is your complete net worth. In the case of poker, or in real life as an angel investor, you would never, ever put your whole bankroll on the table at once because you could face the risk of total ruin.

The risk of ruin is your bankroll going to zero and you having to leave the game.

So what percentage of your net worth—your bankroll— should you put on the table? How much of your net worth should you risk angel investing? It largely depends on three things:

1. How tied up can you afford this portion of your net worth to be (i.e., do you need to tap into this money for college and retirement in three years or in thirty years?)?

2. How easy is it for you to get more money (i.e., are you a twenty-five-year-old NBA player with a $100 million

contract and two more contracts to come, or are you a sixty-five-year-old retiree with $10 million in net worth?)?

3. How would you feel if you lost 100 percent of the money you allocated to angel investing?

If you love taking risks and don't mind being locked up for a decade, I could see you putting 10 to 20 percent of your bankroll into angel investing. If you can tolerate risk, but don't love it, and you can handle being illiquid for a decade, I could see you putting 5 percent of your bankroll into angel investing.

If you were learning how to play poker, would you sit at the $100,000 buy-in table with a bunch of sharks or would you play at the $100 buy-in table for a couple of months until you were a winner?

That's what I'm advocating here: use this process to learn the game.

If you put only about 2 percent of your chip stack to work ($25,000) on your first ten angel investments, and your chip stack is only 15 percent of your net worth (i.e., you allocated $1.5 million of your $10 million net worth to angel investing), well, if your first ten deals return zero, you've lost only $25,000 of $10 million—or 0.25 percent of your net worth. If your bond portfolio or the stock market returns 4 percent a year, you will recoup that loss in a month.

If your net worth is only $1 million and you lose the $25,000, well, you've lost 2.5 percent of your net worth—which the stock market or bond portfolio would pay you back in just over half a year.

In either case, you should invest only to the point that you're still able to weather the "storm."

HOW TO ACT IN A SYNDICATE

As a member of an angel syndicate, you are ceding control to the syndicate lead, but that doesn't mean you have to be passive.

In fact, you can and should behave as if you are directly investing in the company. What being part of a syndicate means is that the founder of the startup has chosen to take on a collection of smaller investors who are listed on their cap table as one entity, represented by one lead investor.

The upside for the founder, outside of the money, is that they only have to get signatures from the lead when it comes time to make important decisions for the company, like when they need to get approval for a bridge round or a sale.

In my experience, founders who opt in to doing syndicates see great value in the fifty or so angels that invest in an angel syndicate. Founders love hearing from investors, even ones who have put as little as $2,500 into a deal.

If you're able to put $2,500 into a deal, you're probably able to "add a zero" and put $25,000 into the next round, and savvy founders know this.

Also, as a syndicate member, you can easily do important things like retweet a news story about the company, provide introductions to potential employees or customers via your LinkedIn network, or help advise them on something you have expertise in like sales or marketing or copywriting.

In short, you should look at angel investing as a competition where you're trying to provide more value than any other angel in the company—including me!

Good luck with that, because I've developed an entire platform over twenty-plus years to help founders, something you can replicate—or exceed—but that will take another book, which I'm willing to write if you're willing to do the work and be an angel investor.

Good luck with that, though, because I've got a two-decade head start and I've built an entire platform for helping founders. But hey, records are made to be broken, right?

WRITE DEAL MEMOS

For all ten of the startups you select, you need to write a "deal memo" explaining why you're investing, what you think the risks are, and what you think has to go right for the startup to return money on your investment.

You will review these deal memos every time the startup raises a new round of funding so that you can test if your original thesis still applies. What you'll undoubtedly learn is that no one knows exactly how or why a startup breaks out, but there are trends—especially in how *you* think.

For every startup you didn't invest in, write clear notes on the reasons why you passed. You will look back on these notes and learn exactly how bad you were at this, and over time see how much better you've gotten.

Even when you are investing in a startup via a syndicate, I recommend you meet in person with the founders at least once—if not twice. Visiting their office, even if it's a dump, is advisable.

You can really get a sense for a company if you go to their office. Are they wasting money on expensive chairs and tables or are they sitting on folding chairs and using wooden doors on horses as tables like Amazon.com did?

Most important, you should only invest in these ten startups if you would buy stock in the founders themselves. I explain this in more detail in chapter 17.

JEDI POKER

Syndicates are your Dagobah, a place where you can learn from other angel masters without losing a limb or your head. Go ahead and ask the syndicate lead why they are investing, meet with the founders, and talk to their customers—learn how to hold a lightsaber without cutting your fingers off.

When I started playing poker in Los Angeles around 2004, I knew I was but a padawan and not ready to face a Jedi Knight. So, I would go to the $1 and $2 poker table at Hollywood Park, where old ladies wager their social security checks.

I knew these old biddies were conservative and smart. They had played poker six days a week for ten hours a day for years.

I would buy $40 in chips, or twenty big blinds (the $2 in the $1/$2 game), and proceed to play in what I called "Jedi mode."

When the action was on me, I would look down at my cards and peel them up with my thumb covering the top corner so I didn't know what my two hole card was. The ladies thought I was considering my cards when, in fact, the only thing I was considering was what they were holding and what they were likely to do if I bet.

I was playing completely blind!

This disadvantage, like Luke Skywalker wearing his helmet with the blast shield lowered during his lightsaber training at Obi-Wan's command, forced me to rely on other information: the expressions on the biddies' faces and their reactions to my bets.

For weeks and weeks, I would lose my $40 buy-in three or four times. I probably lost two or three thousand dollars to those ladies before figuring out the finer points of poker—which I then deployed in the biggest poker games on the West Coast: $200 and $400 no-limit hold'em, with a $25,000 buy-in.

When I started I played poker and lost with $40 on the table in front of me. Now I've played poker and won with $200,000 on the table in front of me.

If you're going to be a great angel investor, start at the small tables while you learn—there is no rush. Every year, billion-dollar companies are created, and that will continue for the rest of our lives—unless, of course, one of these startups figures out how to make us live for two hundred years, in which case you might live to see the era where a trillion-dollar company is made every year.

If you're doing deal memos, office visits, and talking to customers when investing $2,500, you're going to be a powerful Jedi by the time I'm finished training you. I know angels who invest $50,000 without ever meeting the founders of a startup in person, let alone writing a deal memo or visiting their offices.

ANGEL: IT'S NOT JUST A JOB

As far as I'm concerned, angel investing is a vocation or a calling. It's like teaching or being a Jedi. You should take it seriously because your actions can help create massive change in the world.

A couple of angel investors backed Tesla and Tesla forced the world to take a second look at electric cars.

A couple of angels backed Twitter and revolutions all around the world—and here in the United States—have been started, accelerated, and recognized because of a simple tweet.

MY BIGGEST MISS: TWITTER

I passed on investing in Twitter because I was, at the time, a founder of companies. I stupidly thought that the best investment I could make was in my own company.

One Sunday I went to brunch with Evan Williams and Biz Stone and they showed me how Twitter worked.

"Go ahead and send the number I gave you a text message describing what you're eating right now and Biz and I will do the same," said Ev.

My BlackBerry vibrated and it showed me that Ev was eating some tofu scramble and Biz was having pancakes.

"Ev, no one cares what Biz is eating. This is kinda stupid. Every text costs money. They're only used for important messages and emergencies."

Evan and Biz then explained to me exactly how the system would work, and that eventually the messages would be free and come via the web and that they would cut deals with the carriers to make money from the text messages—it was a revenue stream!

I didn't see it, because I was a blogging snob. I had sold my blogging company, Weblogs, Inc., to AOL for $30 million shortly before Twitter was invented and I thought I knew better than anyone how this shit worked.

My berating continued: "Ev, let me explain something to you. You took the most important part of a blog post—the body of the post, the contents—and you removed it, leaving only the subject line. Every idiot in the world will now think they are a blogger and they will be on even footing with all the other writers, except now we'll all be writing headlines!"

Ev explained to me exactly why I was wrong, but I cut him off and told him, "No, Ev, you're wrong and I would never, ever invest in something as inane and pointless as Twitter."

That was a $50 million mistake.

Fifty. Million. Dollars.

It was at that point I realized that I didn't need to know if the idea would be successful. I only needed to know if the person would be.

It was clear as day to me that whatever Ev worked on would be successful, but my own ego and my need to be right and understand everything got in the way of me hitting my first big home run.

Since then, I've stopped trying to understand what will work and what won't, and instead I use my Jedi powers to understand how strong the Force is in the founder.

I'm here so you don't repeat my mistakes.

Especially not the $50 million ones.

CHAPTER 13

MONTH TWO: THIRTY DAYS OF ANGEL AND FOUNDER MEETINGS

BUILDING YOUR NETWORK

After doing ten syndicate deals, you're ready to build your network with the supreme knowledge that you can now introduce yourself like this: "Hello, I'm Jane Smith and I'm an angel investor in ten new startups with angel investors including Chris Sacca, Jason Calacanis, Cyan Banister, Naval Ravikant, and Gil Penchina."

You've arrived!

That was easy, wasn't it? For a fraction of the cost of going to business school, you are now deep in the angel investing game, except no one knows you. We're going to change all that by setting up two meetings a day over the next thirty days.

MEET TWELVE ANGELS

The best deals are typically not on platforms like AngelList or at incubators like Y Combinator or 500 Startups. The best deals never see the light of day. They're quickly filled by insiders who are sharing deal flow, and by elite founders with killer startups tapping their existing network.

This is why it is critical that you build a deal-sharing network. Lucky for you there's a radical new technology that can help you to build this network, and everyone important is already using it. It's called email.

Step one, create a spreadsheet of all the co-investors in those ten startups you've invested in. There should be about fifty investors from the syndicate and a dozen other investors for each startup. That means you will have a pool of six hundred potential investors you can reach out to, minus duplicates.

In your spreadsheet, put the person's LinkedIn, AngelList, Twitter, and Facebook URLs. Connect with each of them on each of these four critical services. When you connect with them, send them a message that says, "Hey Jason, we're co-investors in Evan Williams's startup Twitter."

It will take you a couple of days to do this, but in the process you will learn how other investors present themselves to the world.

Step two, make a private Twitter list called "co_investors," and include all these investors in it. Bookmark that list on your browser and open it once or twice a day, favoriting, retweeting, and replying to your fellow investors' tweets.

Now you've started building basic "social currency" with a huge swath of Silicon Valley insiders by doing about a month of work—congratulations, you're an insider!

The next step is to start emailing the top, most interesting investors in this process. They might be the syndicate leads, or they might be people who co-invested with you in a syndicate.

Now write them an email or send them a private message on any of the common social networks. Here's a good template:

Hey Jason, we co-invested in Company X together. Do you have time for a quick cup of coffee next week? I'll be investing at least $2,500 each into 2 startups per month going forward and I'd like to trade notes. All the best, Jane Smith.

When you meet with fellow investors, your goals are:

1. Figure out what they invest in and why.

2. Figure out what value they bring to startups.

3. Make sure they understand what value you bring to startups.

4. Ask them, "Have you seen anything interesting lately?"

5. Offer them, "I just invested in these two startups, which are exceptional. Would you like to get introduced to the founders?"

6. Determine if they prefer double opt-in introductions or blind introductions.

Keep the meeting short and be willing to travel to the angel. Let them know, "I'm happy to meet you at a time and place that works best for you. I know you're busy."

As in all things, be interested in the other person and think deeply about their answers. Be in the moment and have your mobile phone turned off during these casual meetings.

When meeting with other investors, always remember that you are auditioning. In my mind, how you behave in our meeting should be the peak professional version of yourself. I need to know that a meeting with you is worth my founders' valuable time. Remember, the hottest deals close before most people even know they even exist. You need to make me want to include you in those deals.

I don't want to introduce my founders to newbie angel investors who aren't legit, and in my book legit people are ones who are present, considered, and courteous.

After you meet with each of these angels, promptly email them and thank them for their time. Include a list of the ten startups you've invested in, with links to each one. Always ask them if they are interested in meeting any of your founders.

Inevitably, people will want one or two introductions from you, and, as a lowly $2,500 investor, you will be introducing your founders to two or three angels each!

Now you're starting to provide value to everyone else in the ecosystem, which you will receive back tenfold in the coming years.

Finally, you need to email all of your founders and let them know that they don't need permission to introduce you to other founders who are looking for investors or other investors who are looking to expand their networks. Tell them they can email you blind, without asking you first.

If you are bothered by people sending you random email introductions, you are in the wrong business!

MEET TWENTY-FIVE FOUNDERS

After you've met with a dozen angel investors, it's time for you to start looking for "proprietary deal flow," which is to say, deal flow that is yours—not the public stuff on AngelList, on FundersClub, or at Y Combinator's demo day.

Here are two different styles of email you can try with your existing twelve angel investors that you've met in person with:

Jason, it was great getting coffee with you last week. I noticed that you're an angel investor in Tesla and I think they have a really interesting vision of a carbon-free future. Was wondering, would you mind introducing me to Elon Musk? I believe strongly in Elon's vision and I've got two specific ideas that I'm positive will help improve Tesla's marketing and social media.

You'll notice the template above is not "Jason, can you introduce me to Elon Musk?" While short, that email doesn't show any passion, deliberateness, or intentionality—in other words, you are telling me you don't give a shit.

People want to meet with people who are fascinated by their vision, so take a moment to state why you think their vision is important and how you think you can help them achieve it—because they might just hit reply and introduce you to the founder.

A second email you can send to your new network of angels is the simple and sincere:

Have you seen anything compelling recently?

If you try this with your dozen angels, my guess is you will get leads for at least two startups from each. That sets you up for your next twenty-five meetings, with founders you've been introduced to by a current investor!

You're now an insider's insider, getting warm introductions to founders who are either raising money or will be in the future, by people who have already given them money.

I call this process "reputation in a box."

Now take a moment and consider just how quickly you've gotten into the Star Chamber.

Okay, the moment's over.

Get back to work.

GETTING GOOD AT SAYING NO

In month two, you are going to meet with twenty-five founders. You're going to listen to their pitches and ask lots of short questions and write long notes about their answers. When they ask you if you're in, you're going to tell them that you need some time to come to a decision.

Again, never say yes in a meeting. Let them know that you need to do research and think about the deal teams. Then, only after you have seen all twenty-five, circle back and pick the best one.

If you're having a hard time sorting through the twenty-five, I suggest putting them into a spreadsheet with the words Great, Good, or Okay next to each one. These are three really easy terms to apply. Put one sentence next to each Okay, saying why you're not going to invest. This is a candid sentence that is for you to look back at six, twelve, and twenty-four months from now when you check your ability to forecast.

Now do the same thing for the Goods, writing why you're not going to invest. For the Greats, let's say there are four of them. Write out why you think they are going to win. You now have three columns: company name, a Great/Good/Okay rating, why you are not investing, and why you are considering investing in the great ones.

Remember there are a hundred reasons why these things fail, so you're not going to have a hard time saying no, and there are typically only one or two reasons to say yes.

For your top four companies—the Great ones—ask for a second meeting and do a little due diligence (see chapter 24). Add a fourth column to your Google spreadsheet where you put your second round of comments on the Great companies, detailing why you said no to three of the Great companies and yes to one.

Put a recurring calendar reminder for every six months to visit this spreadsheet and make a fifth column with notes on how the twenty-four companies you passed on are doing—specifically whether they've raised more money or shut down.

Forecasting is about learning from your past decisions, and you can't forecast well if you don't write down your thoughts and check back on them.

A word of warning: the founders who have gone to Y Combinator and 500 Startups have been trained to set artificial deadlines and manufacture scarcity. Don't fall for it. I can't tell you how many times I've been told by Y Combinator companies that their round is closing next week and that they need to know if I'm in or not.

This charade reached an epic level of silliness when one company sent me a term sheet with $100,000 filled in before I ever met with them. I simply told them that is not how I work and that they could talk to my assistant about stopping by my office in two or three weeks. When they did arrive three weeks later, their round—that they originally told me was closing in hours—was still open.

Shocking.

This part of your angel journey is the opposite of getting into syndicate deals. In syndicate deals, you just need to get ten logos on your site from vetted startups. In these direct deals, however, you need to be methodical.

Next, let's talk about everything you need to know for these pitch meetings.

Once you've finished these next eleven chapters, you will be ready to say your first yes.

What?!

Nope, not kidding.

Let's do the work.

CHAPTER 14

MY BEST AND WORST PITCH MEETINGS

PITCH OVERLOAD

If you're doing it right, your days as an angel investor will be packed with pitch meetings. Like anything in life, though, no matter how unique and special those days are, they can become repetitive—and you can develop bad habits, unprofessional tendencies, indifference, and even outright contempt.

When I was younger I worked on a volunteer ambulance in Brooklyn one or two overnights a week. I started as a dispatcher and eventually became an EMT (emergency medical technician). It was a rush when the phone rang in our headquarters, sometimes waking us up from a light sleep and other times forcing us to drop our bagels and rush to the "bus." We'd fire up the lights and sirens as we rushed into the night to see where we would land on the roulette wheel of scared, suffering, dying—and sometimes dead—people.

It was so impressive to me when we worked on my first couple of patients that some of the older, more experienced EMTs could do their work with a level of calm that reminded me of a Jedi Knight. On the other side of the spectrum, it was disturbing to watch many senior EMTs cracking jokes, breaking protocols, and often being rude to patients and their families.

When you spend time in a role, whether it's being a pilot, an EMT, or an investor, you're going to develop strong habits. To be successful, it's important that you develop good habits and be aware of the bad ones.

Founders always share investor meeting details with each other and your reputation is everything in our industry. If you are helpful, present, and considerate, then you're going to get a great reputation. If you are unprofessional, cavalier, or conceited, or use your position of power in any way that isn't in service of the founder, then you're toast.

Great founders have many options to fund their companies, and your $25,000 isn't any different from mine or another investor's. But how a person feels coming out of an investor meeting will determine whether you're getting in or missing out.

THE BEST AND WORST INVESTORS I'VE PITCHED

When I had the idea for my second company, I wanted to know if venture capitalists would be interested in funding it. I emailed two firms and one angel a two-line email message telling them that I was starting my next company after having sold my last one for $30 million to AOL—just eighteen months after starting it.

I figured if I kept it absurdly short and stated how quickly I sold my last business, it would intrigue these investors and they would respond. The first VC was Michael Moritz of Sequoia Capital and he responded to my email, called my desk phone, and left me a message on my mobile phone within a few hours.

Yep, the greatest venture firm in the world, who made early investments in startups like Google, Apple, Cisco, and YouTube, replied to my email three different ways the same day.

There's a reason that Sequoia is, far and away, the greatest venture firm of all time.

Mark Cuban, who had invested $300,000 in my first company, also responded in the same day. And so did John Doerr of Kleiner Perkins.

Within weeks I had multiple meetings at both firms. Sequoia gave me a term sheet, Kleiner gave me a verbal commitment to a two-phase funding, and Mark committed to me on the spot.

Three great firms, three said yes, and all of them were absurdly quick to follow up.

However, here's where things get interesting: John Doerr fell asleep in our meeting.

While we were doing the Q&A session, John's eyes fluttered shut and he startled right back awake. Everyone in the room—including myself—said nothing. In fact, we all pretended not to notice it, because, well, JD is a legend. This is the cat who invested in Google, Netscape, Sun, and Amazon! He's venture royalty.

That wasn't the only bizarre thing. John had a scratch on his head that he touched a couple of times, and his arm was in a sling. Nothing was broken and he wasn't bleeding, but he just didn't seem right.

When he left the room, one of his partners pulled me aside and apologized. He told me John had taken a spill on his bike that morning and was bruised up. He was on pain medication and his partners asked him not to come to the office, but he did anyway.

Holy. Fucking. Shit.

In spite of a bike crash, JD showed up for my pitch meeting on pain meds. That's why he's a billionaire!

Now, as I was wrapping up this investment, a smaller firm, which I was told passed on the Google investment that Sequoia had made, got wind that I was closing a deal with Sequoia from one of my angel investors. Let's call them "Extra Ventures."

They asked me if they could lob in a term sheet—a formal offer to invest. I told them that I had already made my decision, but I would still meet with them. The meeting with a young partner—who I won't name here—was wildly enthusiastic. He told me things went so well, he wanted me to meet with his partners at their next partner meeting.

Although I was living in Los Angeles, out of courtesy to my angel investor friend I flew to San Francisco to attend the part-ner meeting at Extra Ventures on Sand Hill Road, right next to Stanford University. I figured I could meet with them and then go to Sequoia a few buildings away to visit Roelof Botha, the new partner who would be joining my board.

There was no Uber back then, so after an absurdly early

morning flight I dragged my tired butt over to Hertz and collected my car. I hadn't gotten much sleep and I'm not a morning person, so getting up at five a.m. and all the travel had me on tilt.

As I was starting my car, I saw that I got a new voicemail while I was in the air. It was the young VC who had set up the meeting at Extra Ventures—the second-rate VC firm that I had flown up to pitch.

The junior partner said that he had talked to the senior partners and they had concluded that my startup wasn't a fit, so I didn't need to come in and meet with them today. What?!? My blood boiled and the Irish came out in me and I decided that I was going to confront this partner, as insane and embarrassing as this is to write.

In person.

At his office.

Right now.

In the middle of his partner meeting.

When I got to their office, the receptionist asked me who I was there to see. I told her and even pointed at him in the big conference room where he was sitting with a dozen people in the partner meeting.

He turned white. His partners all looked over at me and he came rushing out. "Didn't you get my message? Our meeting was canceled. I'm so sorry!"

I proceeded to tell him exactly how clueless I thought he was and that I would tell every founder I knew how I had been treated. He implored me to calm down and offered to take me for sushi. I am not proud of my reply: "You're so stupid that you didn't consider that I was flying up, wasting a day of my life and hundreds of dollars, for our meeting . . ." He cut me off. "You're right. I'm so sorry."

I just couldn't relent. In my younger days, I had a horrible habit—back to those habits—of needing to explain to stupid people just how stupid they were. I've since learned that the best way to deal with stupid people is not to have them anywhere near your company and, if possible, not even in your life!

My lobby rant continued: "Here's how stupid you are. You didn't have to cancel on me! You could have simply let me pitch, patted me on the head, and then told me how brilliant my idea was. Then tell me that you couldn't reach consensus with your partners the day after our meeting!"

"You're right," he said.

To this day, that entire episode—both the needless canceling of my meeting once I had already traveled to their town and my own angry antics in their lobby—has informed how I conduct my meetings with founders. Because now I'm on the other side of the table writing the checks—and managing entrepreneurs' egos.

Let's get into that, shall we?

CHAPTER 15

WHAT TO DO BEFORE A PITCH MEETING

HINT: IT'S NOT JUST A GOOGLE SEARCH

You should allocate three hours for each startup meeting: one hour of prep, one hour with the founders, and one hour of post-mortem.

If you're going to meet with a founder, you need to do some research on them. This includes reviewing their product, understanding the market they operate in, knowing who their competitors are, and knowing who else has already invested in the company.

Some of this information is freely available, some of it is in their deck, and sometimes it doesn't exist publicly.

Facebook was far from the first social network, so there was a lot of opportunity for research. In fact, they had a number of well-established competitors, like MySpace, LinkedIn, and Friendster. So, even if you couldn't use the Facebook product because it was limited to folks at certain colleges and required a dot-edu email address, you could still study the space in advance of a pitch meeting.

For Uber or Airbnb, where they created, or at the very least transformed, their markets, it was harder to do research. What Ford and your local car service did had little to do with what Uber was doing, and your classic hotel guests weren't the types who stayed in Airbnb in the early days back when the service was for adventurous people who thought staying in other people's homes—surrounded by their creepy knickknacks—was appealing.

That being said, if you took just one ride in an Uber or—GASP!—stayed at someone's Airbnb for as little as an hour, you would have done so much more research than many folks who invested in those two companies, and you would have impressed the hell out of the founders.

Remember, your competition doesn't take meetings with founders seriously because they think, incorrectly, that they have the power.

Your challenge isn't writing the checks, it's convincing the right founders to cash them.

CHAPTER 16

WHAT TO DO DURING A PITCH MEETING

ONE HOUR MINIMUM

You should dedicate a full hour for your in-person meetings. This signals to a founder that you take them seriously enough to spend time understanding their business.

These days, not only do I take a full hour for a meeting, I leave thirty minutes open after it just in case they keep going. I let founders talk and talk until they are tired of talking. I've had many meetings that last two hours and some that have broken that mark—I'm not kidding.

The reason I do this is that I want to be known for always having time for founders. People tell me, "I know you're really busy, I don't want to keep you." But it's my job to meet with founders. There is nothing I love more!

And those aren't just words. It's absolutely true. I love talking to people about their ideas, their products, and their vision for our future. The only thing I love more than that professionally is actually developing the ideas and being on the winning team myself.

My poker pals bust my balls relentlessly by introducing me as an investor in Wealthfront, Uber, and Thumbtack—before I get to mention it myself.

Here's another way to look at your time: if you take a meeting, it makes little difference if it is thirty or forty-five or sixty minutes because you're doing two hours of research and communication in addition to the meeting. If you do a thirty-minute meeting, you've spent two and a half hours on that startup. If you meet for an hour, you've spent three hours. There is no difference when you look at it holistically, is there?

GIVE THEM YOUR FULL ATTENTION

Now, when you get into the meeting, you should check your phone one last time, let them know if you have a hard stop, and ask them how they would like to run the meeting. Here's what I say: "Would you like to run me through your deck, show me your product, or just talk about your business?"

This flips the script they are used to. My contemporaries are known for dictating to investments how they should do *their* meetings—as in the investor's meeting. That's reasonable— each investor has their process—but I look at those other investors and think, "How can I be more valuable than they are?"

I remember one time I saw my friend Dave McClure, who is a self-admitted scatterbrain, grab a laptop from a founder and flip it around, take control of the keyboard, and start rifling through their deck. Another time at my LAUNCH Festival, a conference where startups pitch themselves to get into my incubator, he wouldn't stop tweeting and was not paying attention to a founder who was onstage pitching. Dave was one of our expert judges.

Now while we are not the strictest of competitors, as most angel deals have a dozen investors these days, we are both developing brands in the world designed to increase our deal flow.

If Dave's brand is distracted, my brand is laser-focused.

BRING PEN AND PAPER

So, when you get in that meeting, look at it like you're being videotaped and it will be on the local news that night. Show up focused, with a notebook and pen so you can take notes like an adult. Never take notes on your laptop, and certainly don't be "that guy" who takes notes on their tablet with a stylus.

For the love of God, never take notes on your smartphone—you'll look like a clueless idiot. Adults take notes on paper and review them later. If you take notes in a book, you are signaling this person that their product and their vision are worthy of being commemorated in your journal for all time.

ACTIVATE SILENT MODE

When the meeting starts, say, "Let me take a moment to turn off my phone."

Important people have the ability to turn off their phones because the world can wait for them. People who are not important have to react to their phones and be at the mercy of people pinging them.

If you haven't figured this out in life yet, it's okay. It took me a while to figure this out.

COFFEE SHOPS ARE A LAST RESORT

It is permissible for the meeting to take place at a cafe, but if you're going to do this professionally, a proper conference room is required. In fact, if you are writing checks and don't have a conference room available, it makes me wonder why not.

Ever since I started going to meetings with people like Barry Diller, who has crisp, sharpened pencils and pads in the middle of the table, or at the elite banker Allen & Company, where they have a button that allows them to call a waiter without you ever knowing it, I've become obsessed with "conference room prep."

In our conference room, we will have fresh-pressed juices, a snack basket, phone chargers, pads, pens, and every dongle you can think of to hook up your phone. My assistant or chief of staff escorts our guests to the room, sets up their computer, and tests it before the meeting starts and, critically, asks them if we can get them a hipster coffee or tea from one of San Francisco's many elite roasters.

I want folks to feel like meeting with me is like going to a restaurant with multiple Michelin stars. I want folks to understand that we are professionals.

I'm not trying to impress folks with expensive offices, but I do want to impress upon them that they are meeting with the best angel investor in the world—even if I'm only in the top five or ten right now.

Details matter.

THE BEST INTERVIEW QUESTIONS ARE THE ONES YOU DIDN'T WRITE

Over time I've learned that your best next question is hidden in the subject's answer to your last question. I've interviewed thousands of people as a journalist, podcaster, and investor, and in that time the best interviews are the ones that morph into conversations. In a conversation you don't have a list of questions to run through, you have a discussion partner who you volley ideas back and forth with.

The more you listen to the partner, and really take in what they are saying, the greater conversationalist you will be. Sure, I've given you important questions to ask in this book (see chapter 18), but those questions are not as important as your ability to listen. Being present and keeping your mouth shut is something that does not come naturally to successful people, but I see it often in the most successful people I know.

I've pushed the envelope on this technique while interviewing subjects for my podcasts, one time taking a live wire of a subject and simply saying one or two words inquisitively, like "solar?" or "food production?"

NEVER SAY YES OR NO DURING A PITCH

There is no reason to say yes or no during a meeting. I've done it and I've regretted it. If you say yes or no during a pitch meeting, you're going to seem impulsive and not considered—which is a bad look for an angel, who should be wise and methodical.

Founders are very charismatic and so convincing that they get people to follow them to build things on spec or for half the salary they would normally command. The superpower that most founders have in common is persuasiveness, and that superpower fades as you leave their reality distortion field. It weakens even more over time.

Good founders will ask you straight up, "Are you in?" or "How much would you like to invest?" Your best response is, "This has been great. Give me a couple of days to give it some thought and let's talk on Monday. I might have some follow-up questions on email as well."

After you do that, set a to-do list item for Monday and let them know if you're in or not.

Of course, if you choose to meet with the founders two or three more times, by all means, feel free to give them the news in person during a follow-up meeting.

CHAPTER 17

HOW TO PICK A BILLION-DOLLAR FOUNDER

THE BILLION-DOLLAR QUESTION

People always ask me, "How do you pick billion-dollar companies to invest in?"

You don't pick billion-dollar companies.

You pick billion-dollar founders.

FILTERING YOUR DEAL FLOW

When I started angel investing five years ago, I got two pieces of advice over and over again.

First, people told me that being a great angel investor is

about picking the right startups. Great! That makes sense, thank you for the advice, I will now go about picking the right startups!

Second, I heard that no one has the ability to know—even here in Silicon Valley, where it's our jobs—which companies will actually *break*, instead of *puttering* or *flaming out*.

How was I to reconcile these two commonly agreed on but contradicting statements, that you need to pick the right startups but that no one can know for sure?

What I learned is that, while no one knows which of the great founders and startups will have breakout success, it's fairly easy to know which founders and ideas are so shitty—or worse, small—that they have no chance of breaking out.

I use two methods to sort through the deluge of startups contacting me. I eliminate the small ideas and weak founders. Then I double down on the great founders and big ideas.

While I can't be sure which businesses will be the next Google, Uber, or Facebook, I can be pretty sure which businesses will not be—and not waste time engaging them.

That's really half the battle, focusing on the winners, the big markets, and the clear ideas.

When I get an email, I never go straight to the meeting. I ask how many full-time employees they have, how much money they've made, their funding history, how they acquire customers, and why they are building this business. The FTE and money-raised answers tell me what their burn rate is and how much they have left in the bank. Most founders think I'm psychic when I tell them these numbers, numbers they haven't shared with me!

If they insist on an in-person meeting, they are either famous or clueless. Or maybe both.

Asking for more detail before an in-person meeting shows founders that you are focused on things that matter, not just taking meetings because you're lonely.

Angel investing requires a level of ruthlessness and promiscuity with your time because the odds are so challenged. You need to say no, or, as I passive-aggressively taunt folks, "not yet," to at least fifty founders for every one you invest in, while understanding that one of your two hundred investments will make 99.9-plus percent of your overall returns.

Let's think about that for a moment. If I do my job correctly, I'll review over ten thousand startups in my decade as an angel—meeting with thousands of them in person—in order to place just two hundred bets, of which perhaps 197, 198, or 199 will have little or no impact on my overall returns.

Said another way, thousands of meetings and millions invested will amount to nothing, while one bet—the longest of the long shots—will return five thousand times my investment, making me the guy who splits William Tell's arrow, which had moments ago split the arrow that had landed in the bull's-eye.

That's angel investing.

Let's keep going as candidly and quickly as possible, because you need to start taking thousands of meetings in order to find your first dozen investments, which, who knows, could result in you hitting your five-thousand-times returner this year!

Someone reading this book inevitably will, so why couldn't that be you?

FINDING BUSINESSES THAT CAN SCALE

Okay, there are two types of businesses in my world: insanely scalable ones and everything else.

Independent films, restaurants, bars, bed-and-breakfasts, consulting firms, clothing lines, and microbreweries are—with very rare exceptions—the businesses that, no matter how hard you and the founders work on them, will not scale.

Scaling in my world means achieving a valuation of billions of dollars, which means making tens to hundreds of millions of dollars, which means my shares become worth a hundred, two hundred, or five hundred times more valuable.

Even if you make a movie that sweeps the Oscars, the chances of me making two to ten times my money are slim. Oftentimes the investor agreements for movies cap the actual upside and, if it doesn't, the studio that buys your film for a flat rate and distributes the hell out of it will make sure you see little or nothing with their creative accounting.

As one rich person I know said, "Want to know how to make a billion dollars making movies? Start with ten billion dollars." Another Hollywood insider told me that the only reason for rich people to invest in movies is to go to cool parties.

Now, you're probably thinking I'm wrong about scaling businesses right now because you can think about McDonald's, Starbucks, and lululemon as examples of things that have broken out, but those businesses were very, very hard to scale, typically taking many decades to reach billions of dollars in enterprise value.

Most of us don't have three or four decades to build our fortunes. We want to do it in five to ten years, which I think is a reasonable window if you read this book and do what I tell you.

If you compare businesses made from atoms (brick-and-mortar shops like Starbucks and McDonald's) to businesses made from bits (software), there is no comparison.

In order for Starbucks to reach a billion customers, they needed to open tens of thousands of stores, which on average serve five hundred to seven hundred cups a day, according to reports. Starbucks was founded in 1971.

Facebook launched their Messenger product in 2011 and reached one billion customers in 2016. To do this, they put their software on a server on the internet, translated the interface to a couple dozen languages, and it was instantly available to 100 percent of the modern world, capable of making them money (essentially, those people with internet access).

If McDonald's wants to make $1 million in profit today, they have to sell ten million more hamburgers to five to ten million people, as they're reportedly making about a dime on each. A software company like Slack, which sells each "seat" of their chat software for about $150 a year, needs to sell only sixty-seven hundred executives their software because their incremental cost of selling and delivering software is nearly zero.

Once you've written software, it costs essentially the same to have one thousand people use it as one million—not so for hamburger or lattes, each of which requires massive amounts of real estate, cows being murdered for their meat or tortured for their milk, and low-paid humans to prepare them and hand them to you with a fake smile and a broken spirit.

Now, you're probably wondering about Facebook's ability to

reach the billions who are not yet online, but the harsh truth is that they are largely worthless as customers because if they don't have the resources to own a computer or mobile phone, they don't have the resources to buy your software or be meaningful eyeballs to sell to advertisers.

Don't cry about it for too long, because Bill Gates, the greatest entrepreneur-turned-philanthropist in history, and his wife, Melinda, are busy leading the charge to eliminate abject poverty in the world. And you know what, they're going to succeed. When they do, we'll have another couple of billion customers available to sell into.

OVERCOMING BLIND SPOTS

Of course, as you get better and better at this, you build up "signaling" that allows you to quickly qualify founders and startups. Of course, you have to be careful that your signaling is not off because, well, the rules and heuristics you build up over the years can create blind spots.

Let's say, for example, you learn over time that the founders you've met with who do copycat products never seem to win. Then you're introduced to Mark Zuckerberg, who shows you an early version of Facebook. Because the first iterations of Facebook weren't much different than Friendster or MySpace, you might dismiss him as a rip-off artist.

And you'd miss out, because the social media space was ripe for someone to come up with a cleaner, more easily understandable design than Friendster and MySpace and a tech team who could handle scaling the platform to handle hundreds of millions of users.

The world needed someone like Zuckerberg to just "do it right," and a guy named Peter Thiel famously gave Zuck $500,000 for 10 percent of the company to "do it right."

LIMIT SIGNALING TO FOUNDERS, NOT IDEAS OR MARKETS

I try to choose companies based on the people running them, not the idea or market, because I've learned that no one can tell the future but I am an exceptional judge of talent.

"I don't need to know if your idea is going to succeed, I need to know if you are," is a line from my blog that has been repeated over and over again.

As you go through your angel investing life, take some time to evaluate the person and their motivations. Ask yourself a simple question: "Would I buy stock in this person if I could?" If you wouldn't buy stock in a founder, you shouldn't buy stock in their company—because there is no difference between the founder and their company; they are one and the same.

Facebook is Zuck, Zuck is Facebook. Sean Parker recognized that Zuck's stock was high and he became Facebook's first president and brought him to his friend Peter Thiel the second he figured out how special Zuck was.

People aren't everything, they are the only thing.

CHAPTER 18

THE FOUR FOUNDER QUESTIONS

A THOUSAND FIRST DATES

The life of an angel is all about managing a deal funnel, which includes three distinct steps: sourcing deals, evaluating deals, and, finally, picking which founders you're going to fund.

Meeting with founders for an hour is the most frequent technique for angels to decide who to invest in, but certainly not the only one. There are some angels whose primary technique for selecting investments is to follow other smart investors, drafting off of their meetings and deal flow.

Another technique is simply to review the core metrics and decide based on those. This can be done by reviewing a deck or by checking public information sources, like the App Store rankings, and traffic monitoring services, like Alexa and Quantcast.

Some investors have a huge Rolodex and simply invest in the founders they already know, a technique that worked extremely well for investors who knew Elon Musk (Zip2 and PayPal before Tesla and SpaceX), Evan Williams (Blogger before Twitter), and Mark Pincus (Freeloader and Tribe before Zynga).

Of course, the "invest in who you know" approach would mean you missed the biggest startups in history: Mark Zuckerberg, Bill Gates, Evan Spiegel, and Larry Page, who all hit the ball out of the park on their first try—at the ages of nineteen, twenty, twenty-one, and twenty-five, respectively.

Meetings are important and free. You should take a lot of them. Ten one-hour meetings a week is a good target for a professional angel. Half that if you're doing this part-time.

My best advice to you as you start dating is to be promiscuous with meetings—but a prude when it comes to writing checks. Don't be a tramp like I was.

I'm going to take you through the four most important questions I ask all founders. The goal of asking these questions is not just for you to understand the business but also so you yourself can answer four critical investor questions:

1. Why has *this* founder chosen *this* business?

2. How committed is this founder?

3. What are this founder's chances of succeeding in this business—and in life?

4. What does winning look like in terms of revenue and my return?

HOW TO ASK QUESTIONS

Your job in these meetings is to play Columbo, the unassuming and always underestimated detective from the classic TV show that started in the '70s and ran for more than three decades. Your job is not to show off or demonstrate how smart you are by explaining to the founder what they're doing wrong or by bragging about your heroics as an investor or, even worse, as a founder yourself.

You want to have big ears and a small mouth in these meetings. You want to ask concise questions that take no more than a couple of seconds and then listen deeply to the answers, considering them with every fiber of your consciousness as you write your notes on paper—just like Columbo.

Listening like this will serve two virtuous goals, the first being that the founder will feel heard and understood by you.

If people believe they are being deeply listened to, they will talk more.

This is why, when you talk to your therapist about your mom, they say "hmm . . ." while tilting their head and looking at you with sympathy. Then they add, "Tell me more about your mother," or "Unpack that some more," or simply "Your mother . . ."

There are six words, four words, and two words in those responses. The last one is the most powerful because it just hangs there, inviting you to build on the topic.

You want to be Dr. Melfi, Tony Soprano's therapist, sitting patiently while the passion and pain pour out from the boss you're meeting with. If you're a great listener, you will be a great investor, as well as a great friend, a great parent, and a great human being.

Second, if you are hyper-present in the meeting, thinking deeply about the founder and why they are taking on the irrational pursuit of starting a company, which comes with a greater than 80 percent chance of failure and a 100 percent chance of suffering, then you will be able to make a better decision on whom to invest in.

Basically, if you shut your trap and listen like a detective or a therapist, you'll be able to uncover the answers to those four questions better than other angel investors.

You'll have more hits and fewer misses.

QUESTION ZERO

When you are starting a founder meeting, ask one icebreaker question to get your subject warmed up.

0. How do you know Jane?

If you were introduced to this founder by a mutual connection, you can quickly establish common ground by asking these five simple words. Listen to the answer you are given and construct a follow-up question based on their answer. So, if the founder said that they worked with Jane, your next move is to say, "You worked with Jane? What was that like?"

I have a game where I try to say things with as few words as possible because it reminds me that this meeting is not about me, it's about them. It also makes me sound wise, like Obi-Wan or a Toshiro Mifune character.

These are the exact four questions I ask every founder. The answers to these questions will give you most of what you need to make your investment decision. We spend the first half of our hour-long meeting exclusively on them. Then we go deeper.

I. What are you working on?

The reason I phrase this question as "What are you working on?," versus something more company-specific, like "What does Google do?" or "Why should I invest in Google?" or the supremely horrible "Why do you think Google is going to succeed after eleven search engines have already failed?," is that it celebrates the founder (the "you") and what founders do (the "work"). It shows that you have deep empathy and you recognize that this isn't about what the thing does (Google helps you find stuff), but rather it's about people (Larry and Sergey write software that helps people find information faster).

2. Why are you doing this?

Again, five simple words that are focused on the founder. When I ask these first two questions, I almost universally see founders melt into their chairs. They relax, let their guard down, and feel like I care about them, which I do. Just like Columbo cares deeply about the suspects he's interviewing when he asks, "So, what do you do here?" when he walks into their office, as opposed to leading with "Where were you on the night of the murder?"

Just like Columbo, I'm looking for killers and I'm trying to eliminate suspects.

There are some really, really bad answers to the question "Why are you doing this?" The worst two answers, which you'll hear often, are "To make money" and "Because INSERT-

SUCCESSFUL-COMPANY-NAME-HERE doesn't do it."

If folks are building a startup for money, they will eventually quit when they realize there are many better ways to make money faster and with more certainty. If you want to make a lot of money, you're better off being a world-class programmer on a very esoteric and in-demand vertical and getting Google or Facebook to give you $1 million-plus a year in stock and cash for ten years in a row. You have no downside, you can work a couple of hours a day, and you get unlimited free food.

If you're building something because another hugely successful company doesn't already have that feature, well, you're wildly naive or, more often than not, plain old stupid. For years people pitched me on startups that were supposedly going to be Google search for news, Google search for video, and Google search for books and magazines. We all know how that turned out.

More recently I've been pitched hard on "Uber for food," "Uber for helicopters," and "Uber for shopping."

While there have been some successful startups built by running ahead of market leaders, in general, those kinds of startups get crushed or bought for small dollar amounts. Summize was a search engine for Twitter, back when Twitter was so technologically incompetent that they could barely keep the service online. They bought Summize to catch up, as well as TweetDeck, a more advanced client for reading multiple feeds at once, but the return to the investors in Summize and TweetDeck for these acquisitions were minor when compared to the returns of the company that bought them.

The big problem with "founders" who build a feature that a market leader will inevitably get to—and I use quotes here for a reason—is that they lack vision. The act of selecting a feature as their life's work, as opposed to a full-blown product or a mission, disqualifies them from being a true founder.

Elon Musk didn't build a battery pack: he built a car and eventually an energy solution that included solar, home batteries, and, perhaps when you read this, a ride-sharing service like Uber's.

It's okay to start small, but it's not okay to be a small thinker.

The right answers to "Why are you building this?" tend to be personal. Travis Kalanick and Garrett Camp built Uber because they couldn't get a cab in Paris at a technology conference. Elon Musk built SpaceX because he wanted a backup plan for humanity. Elon's earlier idea, that no one knows about, was to put a series of greenhouses in space to back up the biosphere— just like the Bruce Dern movie *Silent Running*—which, as an interesting aside, came out five years before *Star Wars* and featured drones that were an inspiration for R2-D2.

Zuckerberg was awkward with the ladies, so he built a social network that would show him their relationship statuses.

Think about that for a second: Is there anything more important than procreation? Not according to Darwin or Freud, so Zuck's lack of game led to the fastest-growing consumer product in the history of humanity, largely based on people needing to find a mate or to connect with previous lovers (as demonstrated by the number of divorces that mention Facebook in their filings).

3. Why now?

This question has been floating around the Valley for a while, and the first time I heard it was from my friend, Sequoia

Capital's Roelof Botha—the venture capitalist who convinced me to become a "Scout" for their firm, which led to my two greatest investments to date: Uber and Thumbtack.

If you unpack this question, you're really asking, "Why will this idea succeed now?"

For Uber it was simple: mobile phones were becoming ubiquitous and they had GPS. In fact, another company had already tried to help you order a cab via SMS messages a year before Uber came on the scene. Their "why now" was simply "text messaging," but that, frankly, wasn't enough. Without advanced mobile CPUs (central processing units) to power big beautiful touch screens with military precision GPS (global positioning system), there would be no Uber.

For YouTube, which had Roelof Botha as its first investor, the "Why now?" was a confluence of factors and breakout successes that tend to be born during these perfect storms. First, bandwidth costs plummeted after the dot-com crash. Second, storage costs were dropping due to this new thing called cloud computing. Third, blogging was taking off. Millions of folks were writing tens of millions of posts every week and YouTube offered a clever way to embed their videos on other people's sites—reaching a massive audience for free.

There were dozens of video companies before YouTube, but they all charged people for bandwidth and storage, which meant that if you wanted to post a video on the internet, your reward for going viral was a ten-thousand-dollar server bill. Instead, YouTube sends you a thousand-dollar check from the ads they run on your hit video.

Dropbox, which launched onstage at the first year of my

LAUNCH Festival and was also funded by Sequoia Capital, had the same "Why now?" as YouTube: plummeting bandwidth and storage costs.

Founders tend to have these "Why now?" insights without recognizing how profound they are. When I started my blogging company, Weblogs, Inc., in 2004, I had a very simple thesis: I believed that great new writers publishing five short, unfiltered posts a day would get more readers than established journalists writing one story, edited by a half dozen people, once a week.

When I had this realization, it was perfectly clear to me, but even the *New York Times* journalists didn't see it. I remember running into legendary tech journalist John Markoff at the Consumer Electronics Show in Vegas when our blog Engadget was covering it for the first time. He asked me how many people we had at the show and I said fifteen. His jaw dropped and he asked me how often they were filing and I said four times.

He replied, "You're going to do sixty stories at CES?"

I said, "Actually they're posting four times a day. So sixty stories . . . per day. How often is your team filing?"

He said they had three journalists at the show and they would do two or three pieces each over the next month. So, they were doing six stories and we were doing sixty a day for five days—three hundred total.

In some ways, "Why now?" is the most important question about the business you can ask because there are so many folks constantly trying the same ideas over and over again in our business.

Google was the twelfth search engine. Facebook was the tenth social network. iPad was the twentieth tablet. It's not who gets there first. It's who gets there first when the market's ready.

4. What's your unfair advantage?

Founders with breakout startups often have an unfair advantage. Google had their Stanford connections, filled with talented algorithm-writing engineering geniuses. Facebook launched while Zuckerberg was still a student at Harvard, and they used their understanding of campus culture and directories to figure out the dynamics of building online social networks that scale. Mark Pincus launched Zynga with a multiyear cross-promotion deal with Facebook, which allowed Zynga to tag along with Facebook as it grew at an astounding rate. Mary Gates was on the board of United Way with the CEO of IBM, which led directly to IBM hiring her son Bill's new company, Microsoft, to build the operating system for their first personal computer.

Said another way, this question is asking, in just four words, "What makes you uniquely qualified to pursue this business? What secrets do you know that will help you beat both the incumbents and your fast followers?"

Sometimes, founders will not have an answer for this question. And that's okay. This is one you often end up answering while looking in the rearview mirror.

WHAT HAVE WE LEARNED?

After asking these four founder questions, which in total are sixteen words, you should have an excellent idea of what this person is building and why.

These four founder questions give you a great starting point for answering the four investor questions every angel needs to ask themselves before investing. Remember, we want to figure out:

1. Why has *this* founder chosen *this* business?

2. How committed is this founder?

3. What are this founder's chances of succeeding in this business—and in life?

4. What does winning look like in terms of revenue and my return?

After thirty minutes and four questions, you're going to have a strong sense of why the founder picked this business, why it might work right now, and, of course, what they are building.

What you probably won't know are the tactical details of how they plan on executing on their vision, including their go-to-market strategy, what kind of team they have, the competitive landscape, and the nuances of their business model.

We are going to find out the answers to those questions in the second half of your meeting.

We also don't know the founder's backstory. There's another set of high-level, deeply personal questions I like to ask so I know what type of person I'm really dealing with.

Is this a trust fund kid who is playing the role of "founder" with his mommy and daddy's money?

Is this the daughter of a working-class family who watched her parents drive cabs and clean houses so that she could have a better life and go to Stanford?

Were this founder's parents both litigation attorneys who see everything in life, from hiring to investing to landing customers, as one giant lawsuit that painfully and slowly winds its way to an eventual lose-lose situation?

We'll find that out next.

Let's continue the interrogation . . . urr . . . I mean, meeting!

CHAPTER 19

GOING DEEPER

THE NEXT FIVE QUESTIONS YOU SHOULD ASK

In the last chapter, we spent a lot of time on the four most important, open-ended founder questions you must ask when you're considering investing in a startup.

Each of those questions will take five minutes for the founder to answer, or thirty of the sixty minutes you have allocated for your meeting. (There are no "quick coffees" in angel investing.)

Remember, when the founder is talking you should be writing notes in your notebook—not typing on your laptop or iPad. If you use an iPad to take notes, you're a multitasking schmuck, so please act like an adult and take notes with a refined writing instrument in a classy notebook.

These things matter. People notice them.

Now, we are just taking down the important facts, including those that might come up in due diligence, such as their previous company's name, their competitors, and the customers they've cited (more on this in chapter 24).

You can also jot down industry terms or keywords the founder uses that jump out at you like I did when "medallion owners" kept coming up when I was making my Uber investment. (I would later research who they were, how they made their money, and why they were a massive inefficiency in the marketplace.)

You should also write down questions you have that, while important, are not worth interrupting the founder during the critical first half of your meeting.

Perhaps you heard an acronym for a technology you've never heard of (i.e., MVP, minimal viable product), or the name of a book that contained a theory that you've never heard of (i.e., Dunbar's Number, the Trolley Problem). Write those things down and ask the founder later, "You mentioned the Trolley Problem. Forgive me, I've never heard of that before. What is it?"

I ask founders to explain to me every word I've never heard of, be it a company or technology or theory. This helps me in three ways. First, I get points for being considered. Second, I get to hear how well they can explain things. And third, I get smarter.

When I meet with founders, they are frequently awed by my knowledge of their business, and over time I've gone from being viewed as an outsider to one of the most considered and knowledgeable strategists in the business.

Even if I lost half the money I've invested in startups, I would still do it for the massive education it's given me!

Now, as a rookie investor, you'll probably break the "big ears, small mouth" rule we talked about, and do the idiotic things I've warned you not to do. You'll probably inject yourself unnecessarily into the founder's answers, you'll interrupt them with your minor questions instead of writing them down, and you'll probably waste the precious time you have to collect the most important information you need to answer the four critical investor questions we discussed twice in the last chapter, and which I will repeat for the third time here:

1. Why has *this* founder chosen *this* business?

2. How committed is this founder?

3. What are this founder's chances of succeeding in this business—and in life?

4. What does winning look like in terms of revenue and my return?

In order for you to answer these big, sweeping investor questions, you need to let founders talk and reveal their true selves. If you are talking more than 5 percent of the time during the first half of the meeting, you're doing it wrong and you won't extract the information you need to make your investment decision.

It should take you ten seconds to ask each of the four questions—well under a minute. The other twenty-nine minutes should be you listening and taking notes.

I trained myself to not talk—which is not an easy task when you're me—by simply looking at my watch and saying, "I will not interrupt the founder for at least three minutes." It worked, and soon I was able to sit silently and take notes for five or ten minutes, studying the founder like a Jedi Knight in waiting.

Bombarding the founder with questions in the first half of the meeting, before you've taken the time to understand the "why," will only demonstrate to the founder that you're a nudge. In the worst-case scenario, the founder will wonder, "Is this investor going to interrupt me and break my balls like this every time we meet *after* we close the round?"

I used to be that investor.

Don't be that investor.

Now that you've learned how not to talk, it's time for you to finish up the meeting by getting tactical and personal by asking another dozen concise questions.

Let's go to the second half, with the action already under way.

TACTICAL QUESTIONS

Here are some quick tactical questions you can get into with the founder so you understand how they plan on executing on their vision. You can prepare them for this part of the meeting by saying, "Can I ask you a couple of quick tactical questions?"

They will say yes, and you can rip through a bunch of these, with a qualifier in front (or back) of them like "briefly" or "quickly," so the founder knows that you just want the short version.

1. Tell me about the competition.

2. How do you make money?

3. How much do you charge customers?

4. How much does your average customer spend?

5. Tell me the top three reasons why this business might fail.

These questions shouldn't take a lot of work to answer, and great founders tend to be able to answer them efficiently. Here is how Airbnb might answer these five:

1. Hotels and HomeAway are our two biggest competitors. Hotels and HomeAway are both much more expensive—typically two to three times more expensive—than an Airbnb.

2. We take a transaction fee.

3. We take 3 percent from the host and charge a 10 percent fee from the guest.

4. Our average stay is 1.7 nights, with a total charge of $225, of which we keep about $40.

5. Regulations are our biggest challenge, finding inventory is our second-biggest challenge, and having a consistent, high-quality experience is our third-biggest challenge.

Now, if a founder answers a question that tightly, you should be drooling. Many founders, and most fakers, are unable to talk about their business objectively—and that's why they have a board, a monthly update, and investors to keep them honest.

Here is how many founders would answer those five questions in my experience:

1. We don't have any competition, except maybe someone putting their couch on Craigslist. No one is capable of doing what we do!

2. We take a transaction fee, we're going to have advertising, we're going to sell our data to marketers, and we're going to sell our software. Plus we're going to have merch!

3. A lot!

4. We had one person stay for a month, and this other host put their mansion on for $5,000 a night and sold it for ten days last month!

5. There is no way we can lose. The only question is how big this business can be!

Being delusional is an essential part of being an entrepreneur, but there is a point at which someone jumps the fence and leaves the reservation. They're just AWOL, and their answers have no relation to reality.

It's your job to understand just how much crazy a founder should have. It's sort of like being a rock star, where you need to be punk rock and take a ton of drugs and trash a bunch of hotel rooms, but not so much that you OD and die or get arrested.

Just watch Aldous Snow in *Get Him to the Greek* and you'll understand.

MY BURN RATE PARTY TRICK

In meetings with founders, I'm often able to tell them exactly how much money they are burning and when they will be out of cash. It's fairly easy to do: you simply write down what their revenue is and how many full-time employees they have.

If a startup called the Delta Corporation is making $10,000 a month selling enterprise software and they have five FTEs here in Silicon Valley, I simply calculate the FTEs by $120,000 each all in—or $10,000 a month—because they might have non-engineers getting $70,000 sitting next to developers making $150,000. Everyone is getting benefits and you have to pay some payroll taxes.

In another American city, I'd put it at slightly less, say $8,000 a month per early-stage FTE.

So, Delta Corp is spending $50,000 on head count and probably has $10,000 in miscellaneous expenses a month, for a total spend of $60,000 a month, which means they have a burn of $50,000 (remember, they make $10,000 selling their software already).

I've also asked at some point during the conversation how much they've raised. Let's say they raised $1 million a year months ago. I can now estimate that they've lost $50,000 a month over twelve months, for $600,000, and have $400,000 left in the bank. They are burning $50,000 a month, so they have eight months left.

I'll say something to the founder like, "So, you're burning about fifty thousand dollars a month and have six to eight months of runway left? Like four hundred thousand dollars in the bank?"

They look at me with shock. How do I know that?

Sometimes I'll follow up, based on the revenue ramp, with something like, "And the Delta Corporation is doubling revenue every two months, so you'll be break-even in six months. With eight months of runway, you don't actually need to raise money, do you?"

Now the founders really freak out.

One time the founder asked me, "Did someone send you our projections and P&L?"

Nope.

It's all very simple. I pay attention, write down numbers, and do back-of-the-envelope math all the time.

I've seen founders working full-time on a startup not do this easy calculation themselves, the same one I do during our meetings, and unexpectedly they run out of money.

PERSONAL QUESTIONS

There are personal questions you can ask founders to get a sense of what they're about. The one I care about most is, "What did your parents do?"

I used to ask, "Tell me about your mom and dad," but that's a bit of a biased question since some folks grow up with two moms or two dads or a single parent, so the best way to do this is to ask about the founder's parents.

There is nothing more bonding between two people in my experience than talking about how you grew up. Sometimes this question will turn into a wonderful twenty-minute detour and you'll hear that someone is from a blue-collar background and their parents worked as nurses and janitors to put them through an Ivy League school. Other times, people might talk about their mother dying when they were ten years old.

The reason I like to ask this question is because it bonds me with the founder. What a founder's parents think of their path is critical, almost as critical as what the founders themselves think of their chosen path.

You might have someone tell you, like someone once told me, that their parents created a legendary company and that they were raised watching them grow it from their basement to taking it public. Would you make an investment decision based on this? Probably not, but you can learn a lot about how much this matters to someone by understanding how they grew up. You'll also learn about their approach to startups.

In Silicon Valley, most folks think that the kids of immigrants are the hungriest and most driven. Maybe there is something to that, but Bill Gates and Mark Zuckerberg came from various levels of privilege here in the United States.

I've watched a literal trust fund kid, a descendant with the last name of their literal robber baron great-great-grandfather, become an exceptionally gritty founder despite having been born with a silver spoon in his mouth. I've also watched the child of immigrant parents—who are supposed to be the most dogged—give up on a startup quickly to take a job at a big company.

While there are no hard-and-fast rules about investing in founders based on their family history, I find the information I learn from these stories to be incredibly useful.

CHAPTER 20

FOUNDER OR FRAUD?

GOING THE DISTANCE

Being the founder of a tech startup today is like being in a rock band in the '60s or '70s. They made movies and TV shows about lead singers and band dynamics back then, and now they make them about startups.

Bill Gates and Steve Jobs were my era's inspiration. Soon after, it was Jerry Yang, Jeff Bezos, and Marc Andreessen. Of their five startups, three are still some of the largest companies in the world: Microsoft, Apple, and Amazon.

Then came Facebook, with the movie *The Social Network*, not only making Zuckerberg famous but also turning his first angel investor, Peter Thiel, and his wildcard advisor, Sean Parker, into legends.

The CD peaked at nearly $15 billion in sales in 1999, then nose-dived due to the impact of technology, specifically the internet. As the revenue plummeted, so declined the music idol.

And while the music industry was looking down, our industry's jester, Steve Jobs, stole their crown, with the iPod and iPhone transforming Apple from literally being our industry's laughing stock—an AOL- or Yahoo!-level cautionary tale— into our North Star.

Steve Jobs created the biggest money printing machine the industry has ever seen, with Apple making more in a single quarter these days ($78 billion) than the music industry makes in a year—globally ($42 billion).

At the time I'm writing this book, it's Elon Musk and Jeff Bezos that founders idolize. By the time you read this, it might be the founder of CafeX or an AI (artificial intelligence) startup that captures the world's attention while solving problems faster than we could ever imagine.

Everyone wants to be a founder, but they don't understand exactly what that means. Being the leader sucks because you're ultimately responsible not only for your performance but also for the performance of your entire team, the market, your investors, your competitors, and even your customers.

Most people calling themselves founders today are just playing the role of founder—whether they know it or not.

Yep, the buck stops with the founder and 100 percent of the blame is on you when things go bad.

No one remembers *how* you won or lost, only *whether* you won or lost.

The results are all that people will judge you on. You can pile up the lawsuits and bad will for years—just ask Zuckerberg—

but if you build a billion-dollar business, no one will care. Build a hundred-billion-dollar business and they will say you're a genius—even if you screwed all your friends and double-crossed your customers in the process (again, ask Zuckerberg).

Being the founder means that all of the hard problems, even the ones the smartest people you convinced to join your team can't solve, are now yours to solve. Imagine you have six people at your startup and every week they run into just three problems they can't solve—one problem every other day. That means you're going to face over fifty challenging problems every month—many of them unsolvable—in addition to the ones you're facing as the founder.

If you're sick, tired, or feeling blue, guess what? F you. Solve the problem!

If you don't have enough resources and your best developer just quit to work at Google? Guess what? F you. Solve the problem!

If your most supportive investor, who promised to fund your next round, gets a divorce at the same time their number one portfolio company gets hammered by a shareholder lawsuit and loses 90 percent of their customers? Guess what? F you. Solve the problem!

Patent troll wakes up and decides to sue you the day after you launch your product? Guess what? F you. Solve the problem!

It sucks to be the founder, but if you're a young person watching social media and TV and you see Snapchat's Evan Spiegel getting engaged to a model and filing to go public, you're going to think that it's all champagne and roses.

I love that fact that people are drawn to the light, even if it may singe them and eventually burn out. At least they tried.

However, as an investor, you have to be careful that you don't invest in thirty schmucks who are not capable of dealing with the never-ending shitshow that is the life of a founder.

Now let's talk about how you, the angel investor, can determine if the person pitching you is a fraud or a founder.

KEY FOUNDER TRAITS

At the core of being a great founder is the unrelenting desire to see your vision—or version—of the world realized. When you meet with founders as often as an angel should, you're going to very quickly be able to sense if their startup matters enough to them.

What you need to figure out is if this founder will quit when things get hard. Anyone can come to work if there is three million in the bank, people are getting paid top salaries, and you have free food.

Will this founder go without pay for three months, cut the free food, and ask everyone on the team to take 50 percent deferred salaries for a few months when the money runs out?

The number one reason a startup shuts down is not actually running out of money, which is what most people believe. The number one reason a startup fails is that the founder gives up.

I've seen many founders run on fumes, take side jobs, and even put payroll on their personal credit cards to rescue the business.

There is a new generation of fauxtrepreneurs out there now, who are obsessed with the startup "lifestyle," and totally stoked to build a company when it's easy, but who would never consider taking less than what they could make working for Google.

If a founder starts a discussion about their compensation at a startup with "I would like to make what Google just offered me," you can be sure that this founder will quit when they get a better offer. Of course, you can get max money at Google given the fact that they have a massive money printing machine and literally don't know what to do with all their profits.

Another huge red flag is founders who won't start working until they are funded.

Or founders who won't do certain jobs, like making a sales call. Or ones who want to have balance in their lives.

The founders who want to go to Coachella, TED, TEDx, or to other conferences before their company is profitable are not the ones you want to invest in.

When I see founders wasting time at events that will not directly result in landing investors, clients, or team members, I cringe. And I take my chip stack elsewhere.

The same goes for founders who spend their money and time on their office space instead of their products.

Taj Mahal syndrome is perhaps the surest sign that a company has peaked. When I saw that Apple was building the most amazing campus in the history of humanity, with a 2.8-million-square-foot spaceship-shaped building at its center, while their phones and laptops were being panned by their most loyal fans, I shook my head.

Is Apple's greatest creation since the passing of Steve Jobs really going to be their new campus?

Maybe so. Damn.

IT'S NO SECRET

One huge red flag is when the founders of a company sell off a great deal of shares early, transferring all of the risk and responsibility to their investors. That's what the two founders of a horrible little app called Secret, which let you slander people anonymously, did back in 2015.

The founders reportedly demanded $3 million each from investors who were participating in their Series B funding and some dopey venture capitalists, desperate to get in on their viral success—which was based on slandering people, and apparently did just that.

Not only did these dopes cash in big, they went out and bought an actual Ferrari to wave in the faces of their employees and the rest of the industry.

Rule number one if you do a big hit is to keep your head down and not do any conspicuous consumption.

When they shut the company down shortly after raising all this money, Bill Maris, then the head of Google's venture capital arm, said, "It's like a bank heist. I think they should return all the money."

SILENT BUT DEADLY OR SILENT AND DEAD

If a founder doesn't communicate with their investors, it's almost universally a sign that they are going out of business (see chapter 27 on monthly updates), but a small percentage of founders are introverts who have their noses to the grindstone.

A great way to test this is to see how the founders behave

during your meetings and to questions over email. Sometimes when people cold email me, and if I think the product or their LinkedIn profile looks strong, I will ask them three specific questions. Usually, I'll send an email that goes like this:

Jane,
Nice start, couple of quick questions:

1. *revenue by quarter?*
2. *how long has the product been in market (months)?*
3. *i've seen a couple of businesses in this space fail over the years—why will it work this time?*

Best @jason

These kinds of short emails can result in amazingly concise replies from founders who are efficient. However, most of the time you'll get a long email that doesn't answer the questions, as the founder goes off on a wild tangent.

These founders, who are not concise in their communications, are probably not going to do well in the long term. They are probably playing the role of founder.

"The empty can makes the most noise," as my Tae Kwon Do instructor's instructor told him—and he often told me. If you're constantly asking for your next belt test or asking why someone else took theirs, you are not ready to move to the next level. The noisy students often quit during the two-year-long experience of being a brown belt. It's the quiet, focused students who move on to become black belts.

CHAPTER 21

EVALUATING THE DEAL

TIMING

When you're evaluating deals at the earliest stages of a startup's life, there is not a lot of data to go on. You can put angel investing into two basic buckets: pre-traction and post-traction. Traction comes in the form of people using and sometimes paying for a product. Pre-traction means the product doesn't have users or revenue.

In the pre-traction bucket, you will hear investors discuss startups in various phases of progress including, roughly from early to later: back of the napkin, basic research, business plan, mock-ups, functional prototype, MVP (minimum viable product), beta testing, and stealth mode.

In the early stages, the chances are greater that you will lose your money, but the valuations are lower to reward you for taking the risk.

A first-time founder with an idea written on the back of a napkin is, generally speaking, not deserving of your funding. If you're a first-time founder, it is your job to build a functioning prototype, or MVP, and hopefully run a beta test. A first-time founder might, if they have a wealthy family, ask their rich aunt and parents to put up $25,000 so they can quit their jobs and hire a designer to complete these first steps (see "Friends and Family" in chapter 7).

If you're a seasoned founder who has built and sold a company before, you can go to your friends and raise $500,000 in seed funding based on a plan written on the back of a napkin, or simply an idea (i.e., "I'm going to focus on educational apps"), but it does raise a big red flag with investors if a seasoned founder does this because, well, they should be able to build an MVP and run a beta on their own.

When evaluating deals in Silicon Valley, there is no reason for you, a new angel investor, to invest in pre-traction startups. You can, but you will be taking unnecessary risk. Furthermore because of your limited time, I recommend that you not meet with anyone who doesn't have a product in the market.

In my mind, founders shouldn't be contacting angel investors in the idea, business plan, or pre-MVP stage. If they are reaching out to you, it's a sign that they can't build the product themselves, nor do they have the ability to get talented folks to build the product with them on the weekends or with friends and family funding.

Is this fair? No.

Is the world fair? No.

You have thirty bullets to fire and this is not a charity; this is a war. You should meet with the best teams capable of building products with sweat equity (see chapter 7) and who have the most traction.

Perhaps after you make a huge return, you can run an incubator for people with business plans, or a coding school for people who don't know how to code, but this book is focused on your investing in thirty startups that will return more capital than you put in.

In my experience, getting in too early is the cardinal mistake of new angel investors. Here is what I see in the market—back of the envelope—and it should give you pause:

- 99 percent of people who write an idea on the back of napkin never do it.

- 95 percent of people who write a business plan never execute on it.

- 90 percent of people who build a prototype never build an MVP.

- 80 percent of people who build an MVP never do a beta test.

- 80 percent of people who do a beta test never incorporate.

- 95 percent of people who run a successful beta never raise money.

Now, put all of those percentages against an 80 or 90 percent mortality rate of startups that do raise money and think about whether you want to give your cousin's friend $25,000 to build their prototype or MVP.

Simply put, there are enough companies that have product/market fit, some traction, and some angel investors but need more capital to finish their mission.

Those are the startups you need to focus on with these first thirty angel investments.

You want the people who are doing it, not the people talking about maybe doing it after you fund them.

PRO RATA

Pro rata is the ability for you to maintain your percentage position in a company by investing in future rounds. For example, if you were to invest $25,000 in a company with a $2.5 million post-money valuation (the value of the company after your investment goes in), you would own 1 percent of the company.

If the company decides to raise $1 million a year later at a $10 million post-money valuation, which would be a $9 million pre-money valuation that pops up to $10 million when the money is in the bank, you would need to invest more money to keep your 1 percent.

In this case, if you didn't invest more money, and the company did dilute their shares by 10 percent by raising $1 million, you would own approximately 0.9 percent of the company. While the percentage you own would go down if you didn't invest more in this next round of financing, you would own shares in a company that had a valuation of four times what it had when you invested. That's a very good thing!

In this situation, where a company you invested in is suddenly worth a lot more, you should look at who is investing that money. If they are smart people, you will want to quadruple down and ask the founder if you can put $100,000 into the round, which in this case would give you another 1 percent and a stake of almost 2 percent.

Pro rata is the right to maintain your percentage, and it's important because sometimes a new investor will want to invest and take the entire round for themselves. In practice, if one of your companies becomes worth $1 billion, you're likely to pass on investing millions to maintain your percentage, but if you had the option to do so, you could actually build a syndicate of other investors to do so and share the upside with them.

Pro rata rights are a must and you should never do a deal without them.

Most founders will give their angel investors pro rata rights. If they don't, something is off. Why wouldn't you want your early investors to get rewarded? If a founder has been convinced not to give pro rata, or says you're too small of an investor to deserve it, I suggest letting them know that "Hey, I'm taking a real chance on you, so I'm hoping you will let me keep rooting for you in future rounds by writing more checks. I'm not asking for free equity, just the ability to write you even larger checks as you grow!"

This typically works because, well, it's reasonable.

VALUATION

When I started investing in early-stage startups in Silicon Valley in 2010, the price of entrance was $2 million to $4 million. As the market went bonkers, and huge winners started to emerge, like Uber, Airbnb, Instagram, and Snapchat, seed round valuations moved to the $4 million to $6 million range, then peaked at $10 million, before coming back down to earth at $3 million to $6 million again.

Why would one startup get a $3 million valuation when another gets $6 million? Simply put, competition for the deal. Founders are generally going to price their rounds at the highest number they can to reduce the number of shares they have to sell to hit their funding target.

Founders, too, are perplexed at what valuation to put on their companies, so they frequently look at what their friends raised and try to beat it because they're competitive. Or they try to match it so they don't feel like suckers.

Valuations matter, but what's more important is that you get into the best deals. I know people who passed on Twitter and Zynga based on their Series A valuations, in the low tens of millions, only to see those serial entrepreneurs and their companies become worth billions.

A quick way to understand the valuation is to ask the founder directly, "How did you arrive at that valuation?"

Sometimes they will have been offered that valuation by a "lead investor," an investor who puts in the largest amount in this round—say, $250,000—and who is driving the deal.

In this case, the round is probably going to close because this investor and founder see eye to eye and want to work together. You don't have to overthink it here. Either you love the company and you're in, or you don't love the company and you're out. It's not like a $25,000 angel is going to reset the terms of a round.

If the founder picked a large number, say $10 million, and they don't have a lead, you can certainly say to the founder, "So, ten million is your target. How did you get to that number?" They may or may not have an answer. "We have fifty thousand dollars a month in revenue" would be a great answer. So would "We have twenty-five thousand daily active users and we're growing at fifty percent month over month for the past three months."

A bad answer would be "Ummm, we just picked it" or "Someone in the last Y Combinator class got twelve million dollars so we thought ten was a bargain!"

Another great technique is to simply ask the founder, "Is that valuation set in stone?" and just listen. Perhaps they, like countless startups in the past, will come back to you in a couple of weeks, after their round didn't materialize, and have a different number in mind.

This is a marketplace and valuations can go up and down, but valuations are not as important as understanding who the other investors are, how the business is doing, who the customers are, and who's on the team.

CHAPTER 22

WHY ANGELS SHOULD WRITE DEAL MEMOS

THE BEST WAY TO IMPROVE YOUR SELECTION PROCESS

Venture capital firms invest larger sums of money in a smaller number of startups than angels. A venture capitalist typically invests millions of dollars while you will be investing tens of thousands of dollars. An individual venture capitalist might invest in one or two deals a year and join each company's board of directors until they're on eight or ten boards.

You will invest in five to fifteen startups a year and join no boards.

In fact, venture capitalists look at the startups that have survived the "angel phase" of investing, where products are desperately looking for a market, and the teams are tiny and perpetually under-resourced.

That's why it's important that you build solid relationships with venture capitalists who write bigger checks and work deeply with founders on scaling businesses that have founder product/market fit.

Venture capitalists place a smaller number of bets, so they are much more careful about doing so. I've seen venture capitalists not invest in a company for a year or more, while they focus on the startups they have already invested in.

Another major difference between your process for investing in startups vs. a venture capitalist's process is that you will make your decisions alone, whereas VCs will debate every investment over multiple meetings with their partners.

In fact, the main reason I've chosen to not join (or start) a venture capital firm is that the idea of debating my investments with a partnership is my own personal version of purgatory—it would be my Groundhog Day.

Waking up with massive conviction about a startup only to sit with a half-dozen bros (the investment positions in venture firms today are almost 90 percent male) in a super-politicized conference room and have to make my case to each of them in order to write a check is exactly what angels shouldn't do.

As we've discussed, in the earliest stages of startups the list of reasons why a startup will fail is long and the list of reasons it will succeed is short.

With dozens of relationships to manage in a venture capital firm, and decades of failed and successful investments made that you have to parse through, there is a simple device by which decisions are codified: the deal memo.

Angels don't write deal memos, but they should, because deal memos force you to crystalize your thinking in the short term. They also help you refine your selection ability in the future by reading your past deal memos to see what you got right and wrong.

THE GREATEST DEAL MEMO EVER WRITTEN

The easiest way to understand what a deal memo is, and why it's important, is to discuss the greatest deal memo ever publicly released: a young Roelof Botha's passionate, and well-reasoned, plea to invest in a video startup that was burning money, had come after a dozen previous failures doing the same thing, and had massive legal risks.

That startup was called YouTube and it made Sequoia over $500 million.

In his deal memo, Botha included the following sections: Introduction, Deal, Competition, Hiring Plan, Key Risks, and a Recommendation.

As I've discussed above, the reasons why startups will fail is always long, and Roelof's list of "Key Risks" is comprehensive, including the following observations:

"YouTube faces significant potential competition," writes Roelof, who details seven different types of competitors, from direct ones like Dailymotion and Vimeo, to photo sites like Flickr that might jump into the video game at any moment. Don't forget the large internet players like Google and Yahoo!, entertainment sites, file sharing services, and IPTV (internet protocol TV) companies.

On top of all these competitive risks, Roelof details all of the challenges the revenue model could face, including "We don't know CPM rates YouTube could comment" (CPM means cost per thousand views), "We don't know what percentage of inventory could be monetized," and my personal favorite, "We are not sure how much YouTube could grow from its current level of 100,000 videos served per day."

Now that you understand that there are competitors everywhere and that monetization will be hard, the memo details more risks, including scalability (i.e., YouTube's ability to keep the servers up and running cheaply), "balancing growth" (i.e., what if a lot of people come to view videos but people don't upload enough interesting ones?), and the lack of any evidence of an "exit" strategy, which Roelof sums up succinctly: "We cannot point to many high comparable exit valuations."

In summary, YouTube has massive competition, revenue challenges, is hard to scale, and no one will ever want to buy this POS—did we mention the legal issues?

Of course, even after listing all of these issues, presumably to show his partners that he's being thorough and, perhaps, even as a way to CYA if YouTube failed, Roelof ends with a simple and beautiful recommendation:

"I recommend that we proceed with the financing as proposed."

THE PIED PIPER OF STARTUPS

I have played with three versions of a deal memo over my short angel career. The first was writing notes in my journal. These notes are lost in a stack of journals that I quickly fill but never review.

I've determined journal notes are important for two reasons. First, it lets the person I'm meeting with feel respected because their startup is worthy of notation by what they typically perceive as a wise, old check-writing angel. When Jeff Bezos took notes in his meeting with me and my Weblogs, Inc., partner, Brian Alvey, I felt pretty darn special, I can tell you that.

Second, when I write in a journal, I notice my focus and memory increase, as does my metacognition, which is a fancy way to say "my thinking about my thinking." When I write, I'm Zeus on Mount Olympus, looking down on myself acting out the play of my life, with a massive distance causing a unique perspective that simply listening doesn't provide.

At one point I thought I should write a deal memo as a blog post. After all, I had made almost all of my money when I started angel investing from the sale of my blogging company. I knew my blogging was very popular; frequently my posts would generate dozens of follow-on posts and inbound links. Those links would drive my blog posts to the top of Google search results and introduce more people to Calacanis.com, so why not deploy this in order to get my investments more attention.

I never predicted that the attention from blogging would result in sampling of my investments products, recruiting of talent to those companies, and meeting with powerful venture capitalists—but it did.

It soon became obvious to founders that if I invested in your company, I would probably blog about why I invested and have them as guests on my podcast, *This Week in Startups*. This increased the number of people asking me to invest in their companies. As one partner at Sequoia Capital told me, I was the Pied Piper of startups—a curious reference that later found its way into the HBO show *Silicon Valley*. (I'm sure it was just a coincidence.)

KEEP CALM AND CARRY ON

One of my early investments was Calm.com, a meditation app. I wrote a blog post titled "Why I (We?) Invested $378,000 in Calm.com" on April 23, 2014. The company had, perhaps, five or ten thousand dollars in total revenue at the time, and the founder, Alex Tew—whom I had recently had on my podcast— was a fascinating cat.

He created the "million-dollar homepage," which was a viral sensation. He was a poor college kid who wanted $1 million, so he set up a web page where anyone could pay $1 per pixel. The press ate it up and he made a million bucks.

However, Alex was a bit unpolished as a founder, and every investor he met seemed to quickly pass on him and Calm.com.

In my blog post I wrote: "I picked this startup for a number of reasons, including: a passionate founder (a Brit named Alex Tew who loves mindful meditation & who created one of the most viral things ever: the Million Dollar Homepage), exceptional branding (a four-letter domain name that's in the dictionary!) and solid metrics (many thousands of paying customers, and many hundreds of thousands of free users)."

Looking at the market I said, "Mindful meditation is going to be as big—probably bigger—than Yoga. It's a proven technique, that is being studied deeply by serious scientists at serious universities (http://marc.ucla.edu/)."

I continued in my "blog deal memo" by admonishing venture capitalists: "However, venture capitalists are scared of making a bet on something that's so far left of center. Something that could get them made fun of when it fails ('How's that meditation mumbo jumbo going? Oh it failed, right . . . you could have put that into the next enterprise messaging play, you idiot!'). However, it was clear to me that this will work. In 10 or 20 years, folks will see it as a move as brilliant as investing in a cafe charging 5x more than average for a cup of coffee in 1987 (http://en.wikipedia.org/wiki/Starbucks#History)."

Thirty months after I made this investment, I met with Alex and he told me the good news. The company was on a $10 million annual run rate and they were profitable. They never needed to raise money again and my investment had come at a critical moment for the startup, which he said probably wouldn't exist without my investment.

A profitable app company with $10 million in revenue is worth, in my experience and depending on growth, five to twenty times top line revenue or twenty-five to one hundred times their profits. Either way you slice it, if Calm.com were to be bought with only $10 million in revenue, it would be worth $25 million to $100 million (or six to twenty-five times what I invested in it).

One of my "jaters" (Jason haters) posted to the question-and-answer site Quora, "Was investing nearly $400K in Calm.com a good move by Jason Calacanis? Why?" The jater added, "Not sure what kind of motivations were behind a bit of a curveball investment like this considering its relatively small niche, ability to scale and return potential."

I wrote back to the anonymous asker on April 25, 2014: "The idea of bankers and lawyers doing yoga in 1986? Also absurd . . . but now it's not uncommon to see 15 to 70 years olds in the same yoga class! It's 100% normal. Meditation? Seems strange to some, until they do it and have a massive, life-changing event."

I added a final note: "There is still a 70% chance that a startup like Calm.com will fail . . . that's just math/historical trends. Of course, I think it has a 70% chance of being a $100 million–plus business that will get my investors 10–25x their investment."

Sometimes I scare myself with my predictions.

CHAPTER 23

THE PERFECT WAY TO DECLINE A DEAL

FIFTY WAYS TO LEAVE YOUR FOUNDER

If you invest in one out of every twenty-five or fifty startups you meet with, you're going to have to say no to hundreds of founders. Saying no to people all day long is a new experience for almost everyone on the planet—unless you were a casting director or a supermodel on Tinder.

Very few folks find it easy to say no, but those who do will say so in a meeting with a founder or by email shortly after that. Giving a clear no is the right thing to do in most people's minds—both founders' and investors'—but the truth is that neither party really wants to hear or say these words because "what if . . ."

Instead of saying no, investors string along founders by saying things like "Let's keep the dialogue open" and "Let me
check with my partners." These are code words for "no," but
dogged founders, of course, hear "heck yes" when an investor
says anything that is not "no." Even when they hear a clear no,
many believe there is still a chance.

I've gone through a couple of different phases of handling
telling founders no. Early on I would let founders pursue me,
using not getting back to them as a way to test their resolve. At
times I've been incredibly detailed in my feedback, giving founders all the reasons why I was not investing in them and softening
the blow by telling them to "keep this email and do a blog post
quoting it when you prove me wrong!"

YOU WANT THE TRUTH?

Every time I met with founders—before I was banned from Y
Combinator's Demo Day (more on that later in this chapter)—I
would offer to let founders "take the red pill or blue pill" after
they pitched me.

In 100 percent of the cases, they took the red pill and asked
me to tell them the unvarnished truth. I would then explain to
them, founder to founder, exactly what I thought of their business, their product, and their pitch, plus how other investors
would react to it.

Founders thanked me profusely for my candor, except for the
precious little snowflakes from Y Combinator. Those founders
are like Harvard students, in that they've been accepted into

a very competitive program and were told that they are very special, so special, in fact, that their startups are worth two or three times more than other startups at the same stage of development.

When I would meet with them, I would constantly be amazed at the audacity of their requests and how forward they were. The program is designed to create massive FOMO (fear of missing out) in angel investors who come to Demo Day. The startups are not supposed to take investment before Demo Day, when over a hundred startups take to the stage and literally yell at the audience about how large their market is and how they're going to dominate and crush it.

Dropbox and Airbnb, two of the most amazing startups of the past decade, graduated from Y Combinator, so there are reasons for angels to pay attention to them, but truthfully the program has gotten diluted over time as they raised the number of startups per class from 6 to over 120.

When meeting with these startups, I would candidly tell them what I thought and often tell them that I wouldn't invest at their lofty valuations, which were in the range of $10 million, $12 million, or $15 million—in many cases with very little progress.

One YC company that I thought was particularly interesting was called Weave. When they graduated in 2014, I met with the founder a couple of times. The product was poorly designed but a brilliant concept: Tinder meets LinkedIn.

Their idea was that if you were looking to get a business meeting with people who had a particular title, they would show you matches and then you'd swipe, swipe, swipe on the ones you wanted to meet with. So, if you wanted to meet a designer, angel investor, or lawyer, you could swipe your way into a chat room for an actual meeting.

I was very close to investing, so I had coffee with the founder. I asked him how much he was raising, who the lead investor was, and what the valuation was. He wasn't raising that much and he didn't have a lead, which is not atypical at this stage.

But I almost spit out my cortado when he said he had picked a $10 million valuation. I asked how he could justify this number and who had set the price. He said he set the price based on just below what the top valuation was in his YC cohort.

"Ten million is a really high valuation. When I invested in Uber and Thumbtack they were nine million dollars . . ."

He cut me off. "This is only a million more and we went to Y Combinator and the market is so much hotter right now!" he told me.

"Umm . . . you didn't let me finish my sentence. Uber and Thumbtack's first rounds were nine million dollars— combined," I said.

His face dropped.

"You're not Travis and you're not Marco," I told the founder of Weave, adding, "but I'm sure you will be some day."

They raised $2 million, worked hard for three years, did a pivot or two, and then closed up shop. I dodged a bullet. To this day, I think Weave was a great idea and I would still love to see someone take another shot at a professional matchmaking app that was fun, geographically based, and useful.

After meeting with a couple dozen Y Combinator startups and being super-candid with them, they gave me a bunch of bad reviews in their internal system and they banned me from coming to the next Demo Day—a ban they quickly lifted for the next one. I mean, how do you ban one of the top ten angel investors of all time?

These days, when I meet with founders who are from Y Combinator, I take a very millennial-safe approach. I let them know at least five things I love about their business and I'm not critical at all. When they ask me to invest or pursue me on email after the meeting, I let them know that "they don't fit my investment thesis," which is a polite way of saying nothing.

It's worked.

Each of the precious snowflakes now feels special and unique—even in the blizzard of startups that Y Combinator has become.

INCUBATOR FATIGUE

Incubators are great to attend, and I recommend doing so, but I don't think you should embrace the herd mentality they typically ram down investors' throats. Go to a Demo Day and put all the startups in a spreadsheet, rank the chances of success you think each one will have (low, medium, and high), and write some notes in a column with a date.

Pick the top five or ten and invite them to come for a formal meeting. Now write down what your impressions were after the meeting, as well as the amount they're raising and the valuation.

What you will be shocked to see when you check in with those companies in six months is that they are almost always going to still be raising money and will be, in all likelihood, doing it at the same amount—or within 20 percent—of their previous raise.

By waiting to see if these turtles get from their eggs to the ocean, you will skip the bloody massacre that occurs as newborns race to the sea (more on this in chapter 28).

The truth about 95 percent of incubators is that they are for the founders of startups that couldn't raise money on their own. Y Combinator and my LAUNCH Incubator would be notable exceptions, as they accept folks farther along the path.

New angels should meet founders at incubators but invest in them six or twelve months after they've graduated.

SAY "NOT YET" INSTEAD OF "NO"

These days, I am most likely to tell founders "not yet" when they ask me if I'm ready to invest. It's an elegant phrase that Roelof Botha taught me and it works like a charm. In addition to telling them that I'm just not there yet, I let them know that I'd like for them to add me to their monthly updates.

This gives me the best of all worlds for three reasons. First, I don't crush the souls of the founders, which I've come to realize is my dark superpower. As quickly as I can make someone feel like they can take on the world, my sharp tongue, quick wit, and Brooklyn bluntness can lead me to really step in it. I've told people I "just don't think you're good enough" and "I love your idea, but I don't think you're the right person to execute on it." These types of statements were 100 percent true, but there is no reason to tell a drowning person who can't be saved that they are about to die. You just smile at them as you slowly paddle away, making sure they don't drag you down with them.

The second great part about the "not yet" is that I give the founder the ability to prove me wrong but still include me. A fire in their belly has been lit and they're thinking, "I'm going to show that guy!"

Nothing pleases me more than having a founder "show me," because that means I'm going to be able to make a bet on a stronger company.

Third, I set the tone that monthly updates are something I like to see *before* I give the founder my money.

Life is one giant test, and interacting with investors is one of those tests. Seeing a person execute on their plan over time is the best way to decide if you should invest.

CHAPTER 24

DUE DILIGENCE CHECKLIST

REDUCING YOUR RISK

Due diligence in early-stage investing is the voluntary act of looking into a business or individual before giving them your money. Due to the small amounts of money at stake, say $25,000 from a typical individual angel, many folks skip this step.

At an early-stage company, there is not much to do diligence on except for getting a better take on the founders' backgrounds and reputations. If you're investing in a company pre-product/market fit, well, there are no real customers to speak of and certainly no revenue. If they have been in the market and have customers, there will probably be under a year's worth of data to actually look at.

As the size of the checks starts to increase, the amount of diligence typically goes up, with venture capitalists doing paid background checks on individuals for things like felonies and lawsuit filings. However, as we've seen from giant frauds like Enron, Bernie Madoff, and now the spectacular collapse of Theranos, even these background checks can reveal nothing if it's the first time the founders get caught with their hands in the cookie jar. Groupthink or perhaps even delusional thinking also tends to set in during investing, with people looking around the bargaining table at each other and thinking, "If nothing is scaring off those other three successful investors, then I'm not worried, either. I'm sure if something was wrong, one of them would have uncovered it."

Additionally, there is often a perception that a due diligence process might create an uncomfortable dynamic in the earliest phase of your relationship, just like how prenuptial agreements are perceived as untrusting or unromantic.

As you would expect, investors who have been burned before are more inclined to do additional due diligence in the same way that people who have had a divorce—or two or three—are no longer scared of having that prenup conversation.

PLAYING STARTUP DETECTIVE

I suggest a deal size–appropriate diligence process, which I've been developing over a number of years. Here's how it works. During your founder meetings, you drill into a number of factual questions, getting more specific as you go, such as:

ANGEL: How's business?

FOUNDER: Great. We're crushing it. People really love our product.

ANGEL: How many customers do you have?

FOUNDER: Twelve thousand.

ANGEL: Twelve thousand, that's impressive! Is that per month, per year, or a cumulative number over the past eighteen months?

FOUNDER: Well, that's sort of cumulative, but we include our registered users.

ANGEL: Great, so you have had twelve thousand folks sign up for the product since you launched eighteen months ago, averaging six hundred or seven hundred a month. How much is each of those folks paying?

FOUNDER: We're charging $50.

ANGEL: Awesome, so you are making $50 on six hundred new customers a month for $30,000 in MRR [monthly recurring revenue] and with twelve thousand total, if only half of them have stuck with the product your MRR is at $300,000 total already? You have $3.6 million in ARR [annual recurring revenue]—why do you need an angel round?

FOUNDER: Well, not exactly . . .

Let's take a break in the action here for a minute. At this point, the truth is starting to emerge, and you're learning that there is a different definition of the word "customer" in this founder's mind.

While you might think a customer is someone who pays you

money, this founder thinks a customer is anyone who clicked on the Facebook login button on their website once and then never returned.

While you might believe that $50 per customer is their monthly revenue, the founder has a big secret that is making them nervous.

Congratulations, you just learned your first lesson as a detective: your best next question is asking your last question a slightly different way.

Let's get back to the action, shall we?

ANGEL: Okay, are you saying that you're not charging $50 a month or are you saying that you don't have $30,000 in MRR?

FOUNDER: Well, we just started charging, so we have $3,000 in revenue.

ANGEL: Okay, great, so you were in beta with twelve thousand unpaid users and you're now charging $50 a month per person and you have $3,000 a month in revenue, so you have sixty paying customers?

FOUNDER: Well, not exactly, okay, so, actually, it's, so far, really we've got $3,000 of annual revenue.

ANGEL: Okay, great, so you have $3,000 a year in revenue, so you have $250 a month in revenue, which at $50 a seat is five paying customers a month, correct?

FOUNDER: Well, ummm, almost. We have two people paying us $50 a month and we did custom software for them for a onetime fee of $2,500.

ANGEL: Okay, so, since the onetime fee is not something

we're planning on doing, you have two customers paying $50 a month for an ARR of $1,200?

FOUNDER: Well, yes, but they stopped using the product so we had $3,000 a year in revenue last year.

ANGEL: Got it.

Let's break from the action here and discuss what just happened. A savvy angel investor understands that you have to drill down into the numbers because people will, intentionally or unintentionally, come up with their own definitions of reality.

I call these alternate metrics.

In high-stakes poker games, you will sometimes see a frustrated player rip up the cards, throw them at the dealer, and shout, "Floor! Get me a new setup." In this case, the "floor" is the floor manager (or the pit boss) and a new setup will be two new decks of cards and a new dealer.

The floor managers understand how frustrating or tilting gambling can be, with 80 percent odds of winning resulting in one in five people having a very frustrating outcome, but with the possibility that someone could have three 80 percent winning hands lose—in a row. That's 20 percent of 20 percent of 20 percent—less than 1 in a 100.

Just like "the floor" (manager) has to understand the temporary reality distortion that a player experiences means they believe the deck and the dealers are responsible for their losing streak, you have to deal with the founder's delusions that users are customers or that consulting work is sustainable revenue.

It's nothing to be offended by or concerned about unless you get the sense that the person isn't displaying a normal level of founder delusion and has leveled up to outright lying.

CROSSING THE LINE

That first example may have seemed like I was just dealing with a harmless, overoptimistic founder, but consider the following similar exchange:

FOUNDER: We're at a $1 million run rate.

ANGEL: Can you break that down for me?

FOUNDER: We signed Acme corporation for $3,000 last week and we've got a pipeline of three hundred deals about to close.

ANGEL: So you have one signed deal and you expect 100 percent of the three hundred deals in your pipeline to close?

FOUNDER: Absolutely, we're going to crush it. I just got two more verbal commitments on my way over here.

ANGEL: But to be clear, you have $3,000 in total deposited revenue to date.

FOUNDER: Closed, yes. Deposited, not exactly.

Breaking from the action again, here we have a founder starting out with a very specific, outright lie: they have a $1 million run rate, which they've either convinced themselves is not a lie or they are just plain stupid.

They probably aren't stupid, since they built a product and

got Acme to give them $3,000, so they are probably straight up liars. You can move on.

If you write down all the facts you have and then have your assistant or an associate confirm them with backup documents, you'll be surprised at what you find.

IT GETS WORSE

A fascinating security company once presented at my conference, the LAUNCH Festival, and they were pursuing me hard to invest. They had a charismatic founder and a slick product. There were more people around their booth than anyone else's at that year's show.

They felt like a real winner to me and over lunch at the Battery, a private club in San Francisco for tech elites, they told me they had signed Facebook and Google.

At these meetings, I would bring my former chief of staff, Brice, and have him write down a ton of facts. He would bold all the facts he thought he could potentially check in our diligence checklist, and the Facebook and Google deals were certainly in bold for this one—those are two amazing reference clients!

When we got into diligence, Brice asked to see those two contracts, so we could look at the duration and revenue potential of them, which we assumed would be long and great.

The founder asked me to call them and confessed that the two deals were oral agreements, but he couldn't tell me with whom or when they would close.

This was, simply put, a lie. Oral contracts mean nothing, we all know that. So to claim them as clients before they signed is fraudulent.

The irony in all of this is that if he said, "We're really close to signing deals with Facebook and Google. We're sending them proposals next week and I can send you copies of all the docs," I would have invested. No one is expecting startups to be a sure thing at this stage, which is why there is an opportunity. If it was a sure thing, it would be called a "bond" or "treasure" and the returns would be measured in single-digit percentages.

Years later, the company was still chugging along, had some modest clients, but was trying to raise large amounts of money from non-accredited investors with an aggressive paid advertising on Instagram directing people to an equity crowdfunding platform.

I cringed when I saw this. If it took me some legwork to figure out that this person was lying, what chances would these folks have—putting in $100 or $500 of their savings without ever having lunch with the founder and without a chief of staff to ask the right questions and cut through the nonsense?

There is a reason that financial regulators created a lot of restrictions around taking investment money from the public.

IT GETS MUCH WORSE

The second time I was lied to by founders and almost fell for it was a clever on-demand business building software I had always dreamed would exist someday and that I had been looking to invest in.

We'll call the company "Food Right Now." Their mission was to allow you to take out your phone in a restaurant and have an ordering app know which table you were at automatically using beacon technology—a small device mounted under the table.

No longer would you need to flag down a waiter to place your order. The second you realized your kids were going to demolish the fried calamari that just landed at the table, you could simply take out your phone and order an additional plate.

During the meeting, they talked about trialing the product at a restaurant in Palo Alto that I had been to many times and raved about its effectiveness. They said the manager loved the idea, thought it was a no-brainer, and told them they could either charge $1 for every check or $10 per month per table at that restaurant.

Even now, thinking about this app, I'm in love with the idea and would fund it—but Food Right Now made a critical error that Brice uncovered in his diligence.

When I told the founders I was in pending due diligence, they went and told a bunch of other investors that I was already an investor. This led to a couple of them investing. Quite often, when a high-profile angel invests in a deal, the founders bring that as "social proof" to the angel community in order to get the other dominoes to fall. It works and I'm okay with it after the company has gotten my wire transfer—but never before.

I asked Brice to go to the restaurant where they were running the pilot to try out the system and to talk to the manager.

Brice brought me some bad news. "You're not going to believe this one, boss," he said in his unique deadpan. He was one of my all-time great lieutenants.

He explained that the only "trial" Food Right Now had done with this restaurant was to put a beacon on the table and pretend they ordered from the restaurant. There was never any real trial. What about the manager's endorsement? They didn't have the specific manager's name and they couldn't say what day it was on, but they claimed to have talked to one of the managers on duty a few weeks ago and asked him what he thought of the idea and got a positive response at the time.

What. The. Fuck?

I told Brice we were going to pass on them and then the real problem started: the angels who joined because they were told I was already an investor asked me why I was now backing out.

What. A. Mess!

The truth shall set you free. Heck, the truth shall set us all free! For founders reading this, there is no reason to lie to angels because we all understand that startups are difficult and under-resourced. If they weren't, you wouldn't need our money to fill in all the gaps!

All relationships that start with lies will end in tears.

Avoid the liars. Embrace the delusional.

There's a fine line between those two groups to the untrained eye, but after you've invested in a couple dozen companies and taken a few hundred meetings and asked a few thousand questions, you'll find that the bad ones stick out like a neon sign.

Elon Musk was delusional to think he could upend the car industry by going electric.

Travis Kalanick was delusional to think he could upend transportation by creating a network of on-demand drivers.

Larry and Sergey were delusional to think they could build a search engine ten times better than the dozens that came before them.

People lie, to themselves and their investors and the world, but there is a difference between a factual lie ("We have Facebook and Google under contract!") and a lofty mission (a.k.a. delusion) that if everything goes right, it just might turn into reality, like "We're going to get to Mars" or "We're going to index the world's information."

THE APPEARANCE OF IMPROPRIETY IS IMPROPRIETY

Here's a bonus due diligence disaster story.

Another startup, this one providing services to SMBs (small and midsize businesses), came to me with decent revenue, a solid list of investors, and a charismatic and aggressive founder.

So far, so good.

We met and they had a reasonable valuation and growing client list. I was halfway there and noticed that a notable angel with whom I had done many deals was on the board of the company.

It's always a good idea to ping existing investors, so I messaged my friend and he said the always dreaded "Calling you now."

He explained that the founder had done a bunch of things he considered unethical and I came to a simple conclusion, independent of further investigation, which I live by to this day: the appearance of impropriety is impropriety.

If you can't manage the relationship with your existing investors, you're doing it wrong. Sure, reasonable people can disagree, but savvy founders are able to manage conflict and talk people down and de-escalate. Even if the investor was at fault, I question the founder's ability to resolve the situation.

Is that fair? I have no idea, but I know I don't want to be in business with a person who leaves a lot of bad feelings all around them.

It's fine for folks to bump into each other or even for the occasional elbow to be thrown, just like in the NBA, but no one wants to be a part of a toxic team.

CHAPTER 25

YOUR FIRST YES

IT GETS REAL

After meeting with thirty startups and picking the one you think has the most traction, the best team, and the most established group of investors, it's time to let the founders know that you're interested in investing so they can send you their paperwork.

You're going to want to have a solid startup attorney review these documents for you, giving you a brief summary of the deal and calling out anything they feel is unusual. It will take an hour at most for an attorney to summarize a deal for you, and it's well worth the cost.

You should double-check that you have pro rata (see chapter 21). If it's not in there, simply ask the founder to add it for you. They will almost universally do this without much fuss.

As you consummate the deal, you should let them know how excited you are and that you're most excited to get their monthly updates so that you can help.

Put a quick check-in/coffee meeting with the founders a hundred days from now on your calendar, as well as a one-year follow-up call. These are simple things to put on the calendar and my trick is to allocate just twenty minutes so founders don't feel it's overbearing. You can extend the meetings if you want.

There is always a small chance that an early round can fill up or that one greedy investor will try to take the whole round. If this happens, you can always take a shot by asking the founder, "Is there any way you can fit me in by expanding the round or carving someone else back? I want to work with you and help make this company a huge win for everyone involved."

These kinds of heartfelt pleas rarely go unrewarded. If they absolutely can't get you in this round, you can always stay in touch and jump in down the road because startups never stop raising money. Ever.

You will sign a bunch of documents electronically and file the paperwork away in your Dropbox. You should try to get a copy of the cap table if they're willing to give it, as this gives you a very clear picture of who was involved in the round and how many shares each person owns.

Over time, you'll become good at reading these cap tables and decoding the investing strategies of other angel investors and venture capitalists.

You can write a blog post about the company and why you

invested. Or you can keep the deal under wraps. Either way, make sure that you are never speaking for the company itself. If you write a blog post, it's best to share it with the founder and say, "You cool with this?"

As a founder myself, I've never been happy when investors speak on behalf of our company—unless we asked them to.

Oh yeah, you're also going to wire some money and, at some point, you may even get paper or electronic stock certificates. Not everyone does this, but it's charming when they do come in paper form.

Congratulations.

You are now an angel investor.

CHAPTER 26

HOW FOUNDERS SHOULD TREAT THEIR ANGELS

BOTH SIDES OF THE TABLE

If you're a savvy founder who bought this book to understand how angel investors think, I salute you clever, sneaky little bastards.

You're one step ahead of the class, and you've stolen the next test from the teacher's office—congratulations! Now, when you land a meeting with your dream investor, you're going to have prepped for the "four questions" you have to answer (chapter 18) as well as the four questions the angel investor is going to be asking themselves afterward.

Answering the questions right will be easier for you having read this book, and because you understand the evaluation criteria of exceptional angel investors, you're going to know what actually matters most: your ability to build a product or service that a large group of people find delightful—and indispensable.

Early-stage investors and founders are on the same team and actually have the same goal: to win. The disconnect that sometimes occurs between founders and investors, players and coaches, soldiers and generals, padawan and Jedi Masters, and students and teachers mostly comes down to communication, execution, and prioritization.

In this chapter we will accomplish three things for founders: first, we will explain to you what investors are going through; second, we will show you how to communicate with investors— good and bad ones; and, finally, we'll talk about the value of loyalty.

WHAT ANGELS ARE GOING THROUGH

Angels need you to crush it in order to have any chance of getting their money back and they will be your biggest cheerleaders. They love you and want you to succeed, so you shouldn't hide from them or bend reality to what you think they want to hear. Be honest with us so we can help.

Remember, on average we get paid out seven years after we invest in a company—if we get paid at all. If an angel has a twenty-year career investing and they start at forty years old, then they'll start seeing returns when they are almost fifty— with just twenty good years left to spend that money.

Most angels I meet are salty dogs, broken-down warriors who

want to be in the arena but don't have the stamina and energy to fight anymore. They are backing young gladiators like you because they know you've got a better chance than they do to win.

That's the secret about angel investors. We wish we were you. But not.

Just like the "money" executive producers wish they were actors or directors or screenwriters, angels are in it to be part of something. Savvy founders make angels feel included, just like directors might make a producer feel wanted by showing them dailies or talking to them about the script.

Some of those producers will be industry vets with much to contribute, while others will be bankers who stole a fortune and are looking to spend it. It's your job as a founder to know which archetype you're dealing with and to sort their feedback accordingly.

Additionally, remember that 80 or 90 percent of our investments fail, and we have to suffer through shutdown after shutdown. It's depressing for us, especially in years two, three, and four of angel investing (see chapters 28 and 29).

Want to make an angel investor feel special? Ask them how they and their portfolio are doing.

If we make 95 percent of our returns from one investment and 80 percent of our investments fail, you should do a self-evaluation and ask: Am I the one breakout hit for this angel, am I part of the moderately successful 20 percent, or am I one of the weak, struggling members of the herd that takes up a disproportionate amount of this person's attention?

If you're part of the 20 percent that return capital or better, include your early investors in your success because, candidly, they deserve and need a victory lap. When Marco Zappacosta from Thumbtack or Travis Kalanick from Uber calls me, invites me to a corporate function, or sends me a holiday text, it's like having your most successful, busiest child include you in their life. It's like being invited to the White House after your friend won the presidency.

It's awesome.

You'll note that I bounce around here with student/teacher and peer/equal metaphors because the relationship of an angel can be both. With most of my angel investments, I have a magnitude more experience than they do in startup land. I'm their Obi-Wan.

Often, however, I am a peer and simply hashing things out, neither teaching nor guiding, but rather fighting the battle with them side by side.

Infrequently, I find myself being tapped for advice by people much more successful than I am, which seems laughable on the surface but is actually pragmatic given that all of my billionaire friends started from nothing and they cherish my objective advice as much as I enjoy my consigliere role.

HOW TO COMMUNICATE WITH ANGELS

Send us monthly updates. Or twice a month. Fuck it, send a short weekly update if it's concise—we want to help and we can't help you if we aren't up to speed.

If you do make it past the feasting seagulls to the water, while avoiding the sharks to become a wise old turtle, remember that we helped you get there—even though you did all the hard work.

Cherish us and help us get a massive return so we can keep investing in the next wave of founders. When we hit that home run, thanks to your hard work and our shares in your company become worth fifty or five hundred or five thousand times our investment, don't begrudge our windfall—celebrate it, because it is more of a reflection of our belief in your ability than in our own abilities.

We believed that you would have greater success with our money than we would. Consider that and call us when you start your next big thing. Save us a precious slice of that next cap table so we can, again, bet on you and your supreme entrepreneurial ability.

We are in awe of you and your ability to create massive value in a short period of time.

Now, if you fuck it up by wasting our money on fancy office space or going to pointless conferences, lose our cellphone numbers.

If you can't be bothered to tell us how our investment is going, especially when it's not going well, or you let other investors trample our rights, lose our numbers.

Life is short. Loyalty is all about intent. So if you're not loyal to your angels, you're an unworthy idiot or brilliant narcissist. Either way, go fuck yourself.

LOYALTY

Life may be short, but people have long memories—even if you don't think they do. I've had many experiences where someone has crossed me and then forgotten all about it, or never realized it, only bringing it up after they wondered why I wasn't doing business with them.

Conversely, I've stepped on people's toes and thrown an errant elbow or two in my day, in some cases oblivious to whom I hit.

I'm a fan of being candid if you haven't already realized by the tone of this book. Life is short, time is precious, so I like to get to the point. As such, when someone tries to screw me, I immediately explain to them my position as candidly as possible.

I will give an example here that is important for founders and investors to hear. This is a tale I call "Jason Calacanis does not eat shit."

JASON CALACANIS DOES NOT EAT SHIT

Recently a venture capitalist friend of mine offered to do the coveted Series A of one of my angel investments. I'm going to obscure the facts below because, well, they all know who was involved and everything was worked out long ago thanks to some candid communication.

Shane, the founder of the startup, called me with the good news: "Jason, we got a term sheet from Investor Vic for four million for our Series A!" (Founder Shane, Investor Vic, and $4 million are, again, not the actual names or amount).

"That's amazing, Investor Vic is awesome. We've known each other for years and he speaks at all my conferences and we're good friends," I replied.

Founder Shane's awkward silence was followed by, "Well . . . I have an issue we need to discuss."

He explained that my pal Investor Vic would only do the deal if I lost a bunch of my legal rights, which I include in all my deals via something called a "side letter." A side letter is an agreement between the company and the investor in addition to the standard deal terms.

For me, a notable angel who brings a lot of value and a syndicate of co-investors, these rights are stronger than most angels', including the option of a board seat if I'm the lead of the seed round or represent more than 5 percent of the company's shares, as well as pro rata and information rights.

Pro rata rights are the ability to keep my percentage ownership in a company in future rounds by continuing to buy shares. Information rights can be broad or specific, but mine are very specific, including all key metrics, board documents, and bank and financial statements.

The reason I require these additional rights is because many of my friends will invest in a startup if I do, and I like to be able to help massively if the company gets in trouble. These rights don't actually give me the ability to control the company—far from it—but they do give me the ability to have more information and a greater level of influence.

Back to the story. "Vic wants to rip up the side letter. Is that okay with you?" asked Founder Shane.

"No, but I will say that it's interesting that Investor Vic wants to screw me, your earliest supporter. If he wants to screw me now, on the first day of this deal, I wonder how he will treat you down the road?" I replied.

When I got Investor Vic on the phone, he told me how excited he was, and then explained how I should have never gotten these rights, that he didn't believe I deserved them, and that he would be the one who decided if I got them. His rationale for all this was "When I got in this industry I had to eat a bunch of shit from other investors, it's part of the game."

I thought for a second of how best to handle this situation and calmly explained, "Jason Calacanis does not eat shit." Sure, it's obnoxious to talk about oneself in the third person, but as I explained, I believe in concise communication.

Investor Vic wanted to take another swing at explaining to me why I would need to eat shit and I stopped him and said, "Let me explain why you don't want to trample my rights. I am the point guard on this team. I invest in thirty or forty startups a year and the best of those make their way to your desk and you've now chosen to invest four million dollars in one of them—one that I invested in three years ago."

Continuing, in a very levelheaded way, I added, "If you try and trample my rights on this deal, I will simply not pass the ball to you in the future—but I will pass the ball to your competitors, and not only that, I will take this current deal and walk it into Alpha, Beta, and Delta ventures personally, and explain to Founder Shane how many unicorns they've invested in vs. you. We'll see if my friends at Alpha, Beta, and Delta ventures feel the need to make me eat shit."

He asked for a day to think about it.

He came back and said we should keep my side letter in place.

We have worked brilliantly together since.

The moral of the story is threefold:

First, as an angel, you need to document and fight for your rights. Be candid with people about why they should respect your rights and make clear the ramifications of them not respecting you. In most cases, people will apologize for whacking you in your privates and claim it was inadvertent. You'll forgive them, even though it might have been intentional, and everyone will move on with a deeper and more trusted relationship.

Second, as the founder of a company, you should be on high alert when a new investor or an acquirer wants you to screw your earlier investors. If someone is willing to screw your early supporters, who helped you get to where you are today, what do you think they will do when your relationship hits a bump in the road? Exactly.

Third, as a co-investor or later-stage investor, it's important to keep up the esprit des corps at all times. Building startups is brutally hard and infighting between investors is an unacceptable waste of precious time and attention that we should be giving to our founders.

I've got dozens of stories like this and I'm sure many people have their own stories about me holding my ground on issues. In every case, I like to think that honest communication, deep collaboration, and taking the work seriously win the day.

That's what I focus on.

That's what you should focus on, too.

CHAPTER 27

THERE IS NOTHING MORE IMPORTANT THAN MONTHLY UPDATES

SIGNS OF LIFE

I have a very simple rule of startups that is cleverly called Jason's Rule of Startups:

"If a startup isn't sending you monthly investor updates, it's going out of business."

It's critical that founders keep their investors updated, but as we've discussed, things are such a mess at early-stage startups, where resources are scarce and competition is fierce, that founders find it easier to just bury their heads in their laptops than to confront or discuss their problems.

It's human nature to avoid difficult conversations, and in startup land every discussion—even in successful startups—

inevitably leads to the next set of even bigger problems that you've discovered but have no idea how to solve.

Neophyte CEOs are quickly infected with a never-ending, low-level sense of dread, which makes them avoid meeting with the very same investors they spent months or years chasing.

I often tell people that I get more updates from startups I passed on investing in than from the ones that I gave money to!

NO NEWS ISN'T GOOD NEWS

The death spiral of founder and angel communication happens when a founder doesn't disclose any of their problems until they are out of money. Once I called a startup I invested in and asked them, "How's it going? I haven't heard from you in months."

One of the founders said, "Great, well, except for the fact that my co-founder quit."

"When did this happen?" I asked, puzzled since it was less than a year since I had invested.

"Six months ago," the founder replied.

"Well, that happens. How's the business doing since then?"

"Great, except we ran out of money."

"When the heck did that happen?" I asked, puzzled and increasingly frustrated.

"Four months ago, when we shut the company down," he replied.

I was furious at the founders, but even more furious at myself. How did I let this happen? Why didn't I check in with them more often?

Since that time, I've gone on an industry-wide crusade to get founders to send monthly updates. That's primarily because I want to read them, but it's also because the simple act of reporting on how their business is doing creates a discipline in founders and continues an ongoing dialogue with their investors.

The more concise and professional the updates, the greater the chances that angels will be able to help you, including investing more money and introducing you to their friends as a responsible founder who's a delight to work with.

Angels want to feel needed, and founders who don't make their angels feel needed have lost their most likely source of follow-on funding—their current investors.

You can avoid all the drama with a simple discussion, before you invest in a company, that you can strategically repeat for them at subsequent meetings after you've invested. The language I like to use will go something like this:

"I would like a monthly update from you that includes the key metrics for the business, as well as what you consider the wins and losses since the last email. I would like you to put requests for me and your other investors in the email as well. Every email should have how much cash you have left, your burn rate, and when you will be out of cash so that we can all plan for future raises."

THE OPPOSITE OF MONTHLY UPDATES

My most frustrating investment was an early one in a marketplace for video production. Let's call them "MovieGigs." I don't have a problem telling this story because I think the founders, who chased me as an angel, have clashed with many investors, and their logic in not sending updates was so stupid that I feel like I'm doing you and them a massive service by stating it here.

The company, which solved a problem I genuinely had experienced, seemed generally promising to me, having gone to a top incubator. The founders running MovieGigs had identified that while the video space was booming, making videos remained complicated, requiring many different people with different skill sets—from shooters to directors to sound engineers and editors.

They created a marketplace where you could place your job, be it a wedding video or a welcome video for your hotel's website, and quickly get back bids from various vendors. Sort of like Kayak does for travel.

After I invested in the company and extended the offer to my angel syndicate, the trouble started. The founders felt that they didn't have to update the syndicate members who had invested in their business. They consulted their incubator alumni list and were warned that information would leak to the press. I assured them this would not happen, but they told me they were not under any legal obligation to keep those investors in the loop. Instead, they would tell me quarterly how the business was doing. I asked for monthly. They insisted on quarterly.

The updates were minimal and the business struggled from day one. It became clear to me that not only were the founders incapable of sending updates, they were probably incapable of running a startup.

While I pleaded with them to send more regular information,

the members of the syndicate became more and more frustrated.

This put me in the bizarre position of having to explain to my syndicate members, who are all adults and accredited investors who know what they are doing, why the founders took their money but wouldn't give any new information about the business they had funded.

Even now as I write this, my blood is boiling. If you're willing to cash someone's investment check, then you are business partners and should give your partners the common courtesy of an update.

At one point, I told them, "If your information was leaked and it got you a *TechCrunch* or *Wall Street Journal* story, would you be happy with that outcome or mad?"

"Would you do that for us? That would be awesome!" they responded.

I shook my head in bewilderment. The founders understood that having their information leaked to the press would be great for their business, but they were unwilling to risk having their information leaked by giving it to their existing investors.

To add insult to injury, one of the founders told their incubator that I "breathed fire down his throat" for not sending updates. To be fair, that is a pretty accurate description, but it caused some trouble between the incubator and me.

Year after year, the business struggled. As I think back on my experience with them, I am certain that I made a mistake investing in these founders. If they can't handle the simple task of sending a monthly update to their investors, how could they possibly steer that business to an exit? Negotiating an exit is way harder than writing an update.

I took a moment while writing this chapter, infuriated with this never-ending drama, to send an email to the founders and our syndicate. It said:

[confidential]

REDACTED,

It's been almost three years since you took our investment and you now have a few short months left to save the business. Do you think you could, at the very least, give us the courtesy of telling us something meaningful about the business (revenue, burn, spend since our investment by month comes to mind), how you spent our money and how we might work with you to save the business?

Candidly, you have been the most uncooperative founders I have ever worked with in 150-plus investments and I'm shocked that, with the business on the precipice of failure, you still refuse to tell the syndicate what is going on. We might actually be able to help you, that's what angels do!

I am truly disappointed in you both. Failure is a part of startups, but not communicating with your investors is unforgivable. Is there any way you could change your strategy in the final months of the business and just be candid with us?

Jason

PS—To syndicate members, I am asking all of my future investments at jasonssyndicate.com to commit to monthly updates, and have done the same for all previous investments that have asked for follow-on funding, after our experience with MovieGigs.

[confidential]

A month after I sent them this email, calling them out in front of my syndicate investors, they promised to start sending me weekly updates—about the fire sale of MovieGigs and their meager assets!

REPLYING TO MONTHLY UPDATES

I keep a Google sheet with each startup in column A and the most recent month in column B, the previous month in Column C, and so on. When a founder sends a monthly update we put the number one in the corresponding cell, and when they don't we put a zero.

We make the zero cells red and the one cells green, then add up the number of updates we get each month from all startups, and from startups over time.

It's fine for a startup to miss a month or to do updates every other month or quarterly if they are more established, but it's never acceptable to go radio silent. If we don't get an update for two months, we email them and ask, "Did we miss your monthly update?" This sends the signal that we could have missed it, which is always possible with spam filters on email and the massive influx of email angels can get, but we are also trying to be gentle in our request, knowing that founders are in a generally anxious state most of the time.

You don't want to put unnecessary pressure on founders as an angel, nor do you want to waste their time by demanding they file TPS reports (Google it), but you do want them to know you're there to help and that you take your investment in their company seriously.

When you do get a new report, it's wise to read it fully and send a short follow-up with some positivity for what's working ("nice work landing that head of sales") while being understanding about the losses ("Sorry you lost your CTO. Is there a job description I can share on LinkedIn?").

Depending on your related experience, there are always ways for you to be helpful. I like to pose these as questions, as opposed to edicts. For example, consider these two statements:

"You need to do Facebook ads."

and

"Have you considered doing Facebook ads?"

If every investor sent the first one, the founder would feel like a child whose parents give them incessant instructions about how to eat. "Use your fork, not your fingers. Put your napkin on your lap. Eat your broccoli. Sit up straight. Finish your milk!"

Contrast that with the parent who gives their children a reasonable amount of food and a bunch of care and attention.

Which one is a more effective way to get the results you want?

The latter, obviously.

It's also less work.

CHAPTER 28

YOUR DISASTROUS SECOND YEAR AS AN ANGEL INVESTOR

LOSING STREAK

If you follow the basic system I have outlined in this book, which is to do ten $1,000 syndicate bets before plowing into twenty $25,000 investments over twenty months, you will have deployed $510,000 in just under two years (or eight three-month quarters). I will talk in quarters in this book often because that's the cadence in which our industry works, not just when companies go public but also when being examined privately.

A funny thing starts to happen in year two, around your fifth or sixth quarter of investing. The dozen companies you invested in during your first quarter of investing start needing to raise funds again.

Remember, when startups raise money, they are targeting

twelve to eighteen months of runway, which is the amount of money they raised divided by the amount they burn in the average month. So, if a startup with five team members spends $30,000 a month and makes no revenue, they will burn through their $300,000 raise in ten months—which happens really, really fast. If the same startup raises $500,000, they will last just over sixteen months if they don't have any revenue.

If the startup in this example makes just $10,000 a month, their runway will increase dramatically, which is why revenue is such a beautiful thing, third to only breaking even—which is second to profitability.

While most startups try to raise eighteen months of runway, they often raise under a year, so many of your early investors will be coyly asking you to have coffee nine to fifteen months after you invest in them.

The fundraising process for early-stage startups tends to be two to four months, so not only will you have your first-quarter investments pinging you, you'll have some of the more prepared or less frugal startups from your second- and third-quarter investments texting, "You up?"

Remember, we said the mortality rate of early-stage startups was 70, 80, or 90 percent? Well, guess what? You're about to see some of your baby turtles, ones that have recently hatched and are waddling their way to the glorious surf, get ripped limb from limb by a flock of vicious seagulls.

It's hard to watch, but this is what you signed up for, the survival of the fittest at its rawest and sometimes most unnerving. You'll see founders cry, break down, and even beg you for money, all while their team loses faith and quits to join more promising startups or, brutally, gets massive offers from Google or Facebook that you can't possibly match.

DOUBLING DOWN

When founders from strong companies raise another round, they will simply let you know that they've found a new investor, hopefully a venture capitalist who also wants to join the board, and tell you what the new terms are and ask if you want to take your pro rata.

You will have a date by which to respond yea or nay to reinvest or get diluted by the new money coming into the company. This doesn't happen too often, and when it does, you should spend as much time as possible figuring out what this new investor sees in your startup.

If new money is willing to pay a higher price, it probably means you picked a winner and you might want to consider putting in another $100,000. If this was a $25,000 bet, you will be quadrupling down, and if you did this as a syndicate for $1,000, you will be, ummm, maybe hundred-upling?!

Centupling.

You'll be centupling.

Thank you, Google.

A BRIDGE TO NOWHERE

You will be tempted to continue funding your failing startups, giving them a "bridge" until they can find their next set of investors, but you have to set some ground rules as you perform triage because you won't have enough plasma, I mean capital, to go around.

Years three and four are when founders confirm for you that you made the right decision when you invested in them, but years one and two are filled with only the confirmation that you are clueless.

The bad founders are revealed quickly in year two because they are no longer selling the promise of their ideas, team, and nascent product—they're selling their performance. If they have performance, they should get funding. If they don't, they will likely vanish—and that's why angel investing is hard.

You have to say goodbye to companies you once loved and that are suddenly gone for good.

The bad news comes early and in large quantities, while the good news takes years—if not a decade—to arrive.

If the startup is selling a product or is a marketplace, you have a very simple metric you can study to decide if you should invest again: revenue. If the startup started making money in month six, you can project the next six months of revenue and talk to their customers. You should look at their NPS (Net Promoter Score) (see chapter 31) and use that to make a reasonable decision as to whether to bridge the company or not.

A bridge round is not a death sentence. Many companies will do one and go on to great success, but it's not a great sign, either, because you're not getting new money to validate the company's merits.

When deciding to give a bridge, you need have a candid talk with the founders about what the bridge will accomplish, typically by having them present some goals and what the startup will look like when this new tranche of capital comes in.

Many founders are on what I call the "feature death march," believing that if they just add two or three more features to a product they will break out. Sometimes this happens. Most times it does not.

Some founders are on a "savior search," believing that if they just add one superstar to their team, everything will fall into place. Typically they think they just need a sales executive or a growth hacker. Sometimes this happens. Most times it does not.

Other founders are on a "partner parade," believing if they just land this one key partnership, they will break out. Sometimes this happens. Most times it does not.

What you see here is a pattern. Founders believe that one magical event is going to save the startup, be it adding a feature or a team member or a customer. You have to ask yourself two questions when presented with this strategy. First, is it true that this one event will change their trajectory? Second, is it possible to reach that event given these additional resources?

In the case of the feature, you can see if they've tested the feature or started building it. You can ask how long it will take them to deploy, test, and iterate on. If the founder says two months, just triple it and compare that number to the length of the bridge. If you think this is the killer feature that will change the fate of the product, which is entirely possible, and the bridge buys them nine months, well, then, it might make sense to do the bridge.

You can do the same exercise with the savior reasoning. Does the founder have the new director of sales selected and have they accepted the offer? If so, great, go meet with the new sales savior and ask them how long it will take them to start ringing the register—and again triple that estimate. If they are starting next month and need just two months to ramp up, you can expect it to take seven months before the revenue starts coming in.

If the founder hasn't reached an agreement for this sales savior yet and they still have to hire one, well, that's a three-month process at best, but more likely six months. Add the six months to find someone to the six months to ring the register and realize that you need a fifteen-month bridge!

I think you get the point. The bridge round is more often than not a "bridge to nowhere round."

There are some exceptions. Let's say the company has $15,000 in MRR and that is double the month before ($7,500) and almost four times two months ago ($4,000), and the company is spending $50,000 a month. Well, their burn has gone down from $46,000 to $42,500 to $35,000 in three short months. If they double revenue again, they will be burning only $20,000 a month, so a $250,000 bridge is going to get you to profitability, or at the very least $30,000 to $40,000 a month in revenue— enough to trigger new investors to keep betting.

In a consumer product, where you are pre-revenue and looking to monetize when you reach critical mass, like say Twitter, Instagram, Facebook, and Snapchat all did, you can simply look at the growth. If your product is free and you're burning $50,000 a month but you're not growing, something is really wrong and you might have bet on the wrong team.

PIVOT OR PERSEVERE?

I'm fairly certain everyone in the world understands what the word *pivot* means in a business or strategy context, but to keep it simple here, I will define it as "changing your strategy based on a change in circumstances or in light of new information."

There are many examples of great founders learning something profound and pivoting a failing business into something meaningful. For example, Twitter was a project that Evan Williams founded after becoming frustrated with his podcasting business Odeo.

The chat platform Slack was a pivot that Stewart Butterfield did based on the failure of his video game startup Glitch. Rumor has it Glitch spent the majority of their investment dollars before pivoting to Slack.

It's not surprising that Slack became a big hit, as it was Stewart's second great pivot in his career. Back when he was running another failed video game startup called Game Neverending, he pivoted that into Flickr, which was bought by Yahoo! for more than $20 million in 2005.

It's hard to call either of the previous businesses a "failure" in these examples because they ultimately led the founders to much bigger successes.

Year two sucks, but the later years of angel investing—specifically years three to seven—tend to be filled with good and sometimes great news.

CHAPTER 29

KEEP YOUR HEAD UP

LIGHT AT THE END OF THE FUNNEL

Angel investing without deep awareness and understanding can be psychologically devastating. I've met many people who made a half-dozen investments and who are so absolutely sour to the process that they won't shut up about it.

Like snowboarding, poker, kiteboarding, and love, there is a ramp-up time to understanding that the long-term payoff comes from going through the pain. The greatest love story of your life—I'm going out on a limb here—probably had its ups and downs, but the people who stick with it are often rewarded the most.

The first two days of kiteboarding or snowboarding are filled with getting knocked on your ass and having your body ache all night long. You can wake up feeling like you got hit by a car and simply give up, right before you're finally miraculously able to stand and have the most magical energy rush of your life as you and the board are one, embracing a speed and freedom that humans were simply not designed to experience out of the box.

I compare running startups or angel investing them like being thrown into a large, pitch-black gymnasium with one light switch. You fumble around in the dark, having no idea what you're doing, until you find a tiny switch, flick it up, and all is revealed.

Searching for the switch can take five, ten, or fifty investments, but once you hit it you're going to feel like a genius, and the fear, frustration, and anxiety that comes from investments going bad—especially in year two (see chapter 28)—will lift and you'll have a level of calm when you witness $25,000, $50,000, and $100,000 piles of your cash burn up in completely avoidable barn fires.

You'll smile while your bricks of cash burn, knowing that you'll get more bricks and stack them even higher—assuming you don't give up and you keep learning.

As we've discussed, 99 percent of my time—and some weeks 100 percent—is spent dealing with the dozens of startups in my portfolio that are struggling. They're losing critical team members and running out of money or dealing with deep-pocketed rivals like Google and Facebook, building—or threatening to build—competitive products that they will give away for free.

You've chosen this life and, by reading this book, you know the odds well. They're stacked in favor of people who take a long view and who quadruple down on their winners. They're stacked in favor of the people who are self-aware enough to realize that the losses come early and the big wins come late in the process.

PANIC IS CONTAGIOUS

There is a psychological technique you can use to keep yourself—and your founders—from staying upset for too long, so you can all get back to doing the work.

Complaining about things is a road to nowhere. People who constantly complain are simply not as happy as those who don't.

When you find yourself in a completely frustrating position, I suggest you take the technique I learned from a book by Mark Goulston called *Just Listen* in which he advises, in a nutshell, to talk yourself down from an "Oh fuck" reaction to an "Oh my God" for release and on to an "Oh Jeez," "Oh well," and finally a simple "Okay."

Things seem really horrible when they blow up (see the discussion about Little Bird in chapter 30) or people screw you (see chapter 9), but if you remain aware that you're going to go through some normal phases of grief or frustration, you can accelerate those phases.

These days, when something blows up, I tend to move pretty quickly from an initial reaction of an "Oh fuck!" to an "Oh well" and then to "Okay, now let's focus on what's working."

It sucks to lose, but the more time and energy you put into your losses, the more you will feel like a loser. Instead, you should have been quadrupling down on your winners and spending more time on them.

When a founder is failing these days, after years and years of being on red alert, I walk in like a fixer asking simply, "What is going on?" Founders will typically talk themselves out after ten minutes or so, at which point I will ask the same question again phrased differently, "Is there anything else I should know?"

I watch the founder like a hawk. When they inevitably tell me the real story on the second try, I give them some gentle assurance by looking them in the eyes and repeating back to them what is going on, for example, "Hmm . . . we lost our CTO and we have ten weeks of runway left."

We have set the baseline. We have reality now. Freaking out doesn't help the situation, nor does telling a pilot of the plane over the radio to give you the controls—because you're not even on the plane. I like to get the founder's worldview after they explain the problem and I confirm it by asking, "What are you planning to do?" And following up with, "How can I help?"

This all seems like a lot of work, but the truth is that being a founder, specifically the CEO, is the worst job on the planet, as we've discussed. All the huge problems that smart people on your team are incapable of fixing are handed to you. You're facing assault from all sides and there is no one you can talk to.

If a CEO tells their investors what a disaster things are, they are likely not going to keep funding the company. If they tell the employees that it's a disaster, the employees will either quit or be paralyzed with fear.

Think about it. The reason all these people decided to quit other jobs and follow this founder is because they were swept up in the founder's passion. So it only makes sense that they will be swept up in the founder's panic. A CEO's job is to smooth out the emotional roller coaster. Never let your team experience the same highs and lows you're feeling because the odds are they aren't built to handle these kinds of ups and downs like you are.

As an angel investor, your number one job, in my mind, is to be there for the CEO when they're struggling, making sure they feel heard and that they know you are on their side. Sure, you can tell them where the land mines are and point them in the right direction, but you're not going to be able to take over as the pilot.

If you're relentlessly positive and candid with the founders and yourself, you're going to have a greater chance of success and you're going to be able to remain positive, even in the face of failure.

In fact, over and over again I bring all of my failed founders back to my incubator to tell their stories of failure and what they learned. Sharing their stories lowers their own founder post-traumatic stress disorder, prepares my next cohort of founders for the journey ahead, and keeps me focused on the only thing that matters: doing the work.

There are things in this life that you have control over, things that you have no control over, and things that you have partial control over. It's best to spend your effort on the things that you have complete control over, like your knowledge and work ethic.

If you're constantly learning and working hard—two things that are in your control—good things will happen. This goes equally for founders and investors, which is why my reality show catchphrase is going to be "Do the work."

DON'T SPEAK FOR YOUR PORTFOLIO COMPANIES

It's important for you to understand that as an angel investor in a startup you are not their communications director. It will almost certainly become public that you are an investor in a startup, unless you take specific steps to hide your activity.

The tech industry is serviced by a legion of journalists as well as dozens of databases for tracking investment activity.

When it does come out that you're an investor in a startup,

the press will inevitably call you and ask you to comment on their status. The press is not your friend. In many cases they are your enemy. Almost all stories have an agenda and often it's not a positive one for your company.

Often you will be misquoted and your comments will be taken out of context. For example, you might say seven amazing things about a startup before saying "but they've got some stiff competition." The headline of that story will wind up being "Investor in Facebook warns of uphill battle against competitors."

By shooting off your mouth, you will then have a founder who is pissed off at you. As a bonus, you'll signal to other founders that you're willing to throw your partners under the bus in exchange for some personal press.

When the press contacts you, you are to do two things immediately. First, forward the email to your founder and say, "FYI, let me know if you would like me to respond." Second, don't reply to the journalist at all because writers are really clever at getting you to respond.

Even "I have no comment" can be twisted by a journalist into a headline like "Three Facebook investors refuse to comment on Zuckerberg's fifth lawsuit."

As I'm writing this book, my most notable investment—Uber—is getting beat up in the press and it's putting me in a bit of a bind. I've been a vocal and positive supporter of the firm, but obviously I'm not fully briefed on every internal issue at a company that does millions of rides a month.

The best you can do in these cases is privately support the heck out of the founders and their management teams and help them resolve their challenges. Never engage the press—unless the founders themselves ask you to.

If you see me commenting publicly on an investment of mine, you can be sure that it's with the blessing of the company.

Other investors quickly and publicly criticized the company. That's something I would never do. In my mind, if you're a shareholder it's your job to work behind the scenes to solve problems, not create more of them.

That's not a dig to my friends who like to talk on behalf of their founders. It's just a different style of doing things, and I've found it to be more productive.

BANKROLL MANAGEMENT

If you are managing your bankroll properly, you're going to have a much easier time enjoying angel investing. As we've outlined in this book, I believe that angel investing 5 or 10 percent of your net worth is a worthwhile pursuit, perhaps even 20 percent if you're a younger person with a steady income stream. The key is to deploy it intelligently.

If you're worth $5 million or $10 million and plan on putting $1 million into angel investing, that's 10 to 20 percent of your net worth. If you lose it all or make back half, you'll be fine. If you go five or ten times cash on cash, you can double your net worth—all while learning a lot.

However, remember that we want your first ten investments to be $1,000 syndicate-level swings at bat so you can learn at the low-stakes table, where mistakes aren't devastating. After that, in this book, we talk about making twenty $25,000 bets and quadrupling down on the winners with a $100,000 follow-on investment. In this model, no one investment is more than 12.5 percent of your angel investing portfolio, which in turn is only 10 to 20 percent of your overall net worth. That makes no one investment more than 1.25 to 2.5 percent of your net worth.

Where people get in trouble angel investing is having too few names, say four investments of $250,000, and a quick process for making those bets. There is no rush here, as great companies are going to always be built—especially in down markets.

When you are managing your bankroll as I recommend, you're going to be able to look at the $1,000 losses and not care, the $25,000 losses and say, "Oh well, it's only .25 percent or .50 percent of my net worth," and the $125,000 investments and say, "Oh fuck, oh well, okay—this is not great, but I did quadruple down on this company because they were doing really well. It was an intelligent bet."

Rich people drop into Silicon Valley every day and write checks for $250,000 and $500,000 in the businesses we pros have passed on, and they get their bells rung. Just like rich business people show up at big poker games, buy in for a ton of money, and lose it all when their pocket aces get crushed by someone who played pocket threes and hit their set.

You don't need to win every pot. You don't need to win every day. You do need to win in the long term. Think about angel investing as a decadelong pursuit.

STARTING IS EASY, FINISHING IS HARD

Starting companies is really easy, but finishing them—by having an exit—is really hard. I had a sign on my wall saying STARTING

IS EASY, FINISHING IS HARD for a decade while I was running my own companies.

Founders think getting funded is the hard part. Then they get the wires in and start deploying their investors' capital. At that point, they realize that raising money is easy compared with getting their investors a return on that capital.

It's just like running for president. You think the tough part is campaigning and winning the election, but once you start doing it you realize that the job is even harder!

Angels have to understand that anyone can start a company these days, given that servers, software, and bandwidth have become commoditized, costing next to nothing, while designing a decent product with a small number of people is easy, too. Heck, even acquiring a couple dozen customers is easy, given the massive scale and targeting ability of advertising networks like Facebook and Google.

You could make a Twitter clone and get to a thousand users in two weeks and build the chat software Slack in half that time. Starting these projects is now thousands of dollars and a couple of weeks, but getting them to a meaningful exit is millions of dollars and many more years.

LEARNING FROM FAILURE

If you come to Silicon Valley and invest in thirty startups over two years and make this your half-time or full-time job, reflecting on the wins and losses, spending time with other investors and founders, you're going to learn a ton. If you're smart, you will read this book before you start investing, after you invest in ten startups, and again when you hit twenty, because the lessons I outline here, collected over a hundred-plus investments and twenty-five years in the industry, are simultaneously timeless and ever-changing.

What worked when I started investing, when there were one-tenth as many startups being formed every year, doesn't work today. It was wise to invest in great teams, pre-product back then, where today you almost universally want to wait for the founders to finish their product and get to market before investing.

In another five to ten years, things will change again, and the only way to understand where the market is going will be to study not just the market winners but the market failures—along with doing a postmortem on your own forecasting and behavior.

You don't have to obsess over the losers, but I would certainly meditate on them and look for patterns. I was able to fix some leaks in my investment strategy by doing this. The biggest leak in my early years was that I frequently assumed that if I, or my very qualified friends, could execute on a plan, then my investments could, too. I assumed that all founders were dogged and die-hard, but I learned the hard way—after a half-dozen startups gave up and gave their investors five to fifty cents on the dollar back—that not everyone is die-hard.

Sometimes in life, you have to go through it to get to it.

That's angel investing.

CHAPTER 30

EXITS: GREAT COMPANIES ARE BOUGHT, NOT SOLD

HOW YOU GET PAID

There are three ways in which angels make money from investing in a startup. They all involve the selling of the shares you bought to another party down the road, and it can happen voluntarily or involuntarily.

The best, but least common, way for you to sell your shares is almost always if your startup gets so big that it has an initial public offering. When an IPO happens, your previously illiquid shares, which lived on a spreadsheet at the company, are magically transferred into your E-Trade, Charles Schwab, or—ideally—Wealthfront account (see chapter 9; I'm an advisor).

These shares are typically locked up for the first six months you own them, but after that "lockup period" you can do what you want with them without the permission of the company, other investors, or the founder. You can hold them or sell them, but they're almost as good as cash at this point.

Should you sell them or hold them after an IPO? Well, like every financial decision, that depends on your station in life, your risk tolerance, and the strength and potential of the company.

If you were an investor in Google or Facebook, your net worth was likely 99-plus percent tied to a single stock, which is scary as hell. One friend of mine sold all of his shares when Facebook stumbled after its $38-a-share IPO, selling his shares in the high teens, only to see it go up a multiple of five in the next couple of years. In this case, it was the difference between being worth hundreds of millions of dollars or billions. Now there's a high-class problem if there ever was one.

In other cases, such as Twitter, friends of mine sold their shares at the peak of $69 a share in 2014, while others rode them down to $15 a share in 2016—just twenty-four short months later.

If you were a Facebook or Twitter holder with 90-plus percent in those two companies, there was an obviously sound investment thesis you should have followed: diversification. If you are bullish on technology, which if you're reading this book or were born in the years from 1960 to today you should be, you should have taken your $100 million in shares of Twitter and put it into the top five technology stocks you liked, including Facebook, Amazon, Netflix, and Google (the FANGs, as we call them). You would have been in much better shape.

Everyone in Silicon Valley knows that the FANGs were sharper than Twitter, so moving 80 percent of your Twitter holdings at the IPO price, or anytime during its massive run-up right after, split up evenly among these titans, would have been very smart.

You didn't have to be some genius to know that the FANGs were better run than Twitter; you need only look at the revenue and user growth to understand that.

At the time of the writing of this book, there are many Snapchat investors about to see their massive returns become liquid for the first time in years. They, too, should answer the question: Is Snapchat as well run, fast-growing, and priced as well as the FANGs? If it were me, I would diversify quickly because in ten or twenty years, folks at Snapchat might be gone—but the FANGs will not be.

I've known a lot of paper millionaires who have gotten crushed because they never sold shares or diversified when they could. In fact, there is a chance that the author of this book could see his net worth collapse or soar in the future based on a single stock or two.

SECONDARY SHARES

An amazing thing happened given the massive growth of Twitter and Facebook in the 2007–10 era: a market for selling private company shares emerged. The reasons for this are (1) the perfect storm of private companies not wanting to go public too soon and (2) the availability of massive pools of private funds from private equity and late-stage venture capital firms wanting to own significant positions in those companies.

While many angels and venture capitalists resisted the idea of letting founders cash out early, they quickly learned that allowing them to sell off $5 million or $10 million's worth of their equity took a great deal of pressure off these broke, first-time management teams.

A person with $10,000 in their bank account and a $10,000-a-month nut is in a constant state of low- to medium-grade pressure, but a person with $3 million or $7 million—after paying their taxes—has enough to buy a loft and take a first-class vacation with their family every year. They don't need to worry about what they spend on dinner, clothes, or vacations anymore and have enough "idiot insurance" to feel like they are ahead of the game.

Now, if a founder sells $20 million, $50 million, or $100 million in private stock, like some have, you get into a very dangerous place, as they are likely to start buying homes, planes, and boats, which leads to massive cognitive overhead. A $10,000-a-month nut suddenly turns into $100,000 and they are back to square one, worrying about how they can afford their exorbitant lifestyle.

Angel investors have been able to access these deals much more easily and I have taken advantage of the opportunity to diversify my holdings from time to time. If you have a winner and it's surging, it's tough to sell knowing that your equity is likely to grow. But taking 10 or 20 or 30 percent of your winnings off your table at a high-enough price and putting it back into your portfolio will almost always help you sleep better.

If you owned $10 million in a high-growth startup and sold 20 percent of your holdings and it increased five times from when you did, you would have missed out on an additional $42 million ($2 million from your early shares and $40 million from your $8 million stake that you didn't sell going five times) vs. $50 million if you risked it all.

If you were broke at the time, the $2 million would have taken a lot of pressure off you. If the company completely imploded, like Theranos, or got whacked for an 80 percent loss, like Zynga did after their IPO, you would feel really smart having locked in those gains instead of getting zero.

Some of my best nights playing poker are not the ones where I win $50,000. They're the nights when I claw my way back from being down $50,000 and leaving the table up $5,000.

M&A ALL DAY

The third, and most common way, an angel makes their money is when a startup is bought. This is a double-edged sword because most of the time a company sells it's because it can't make it on its own. We discussed the horribly early sale of YouTube to Google. While it made Sequoia Capital over $500 million and returned more than the entire fund it was a member of, it was a bittersweet day for investors.

If YouTube had stuck it out, there is no doubt the firm would be worth north of $75 billion, and I personally believe that number would be $150 billion based on the premium the market assigns to category leaders.

Instead of Sequoia making $500 million on YouTube, they should have made $50 billion.

There are three types of M&A (merger and acquisition) deals: acquihires (a.k.a. fire sales), appropriate acquisitions, and premium sales. The term "acquihire" is a combination of "acquisition" and "hire," and it's what you call it when a big company buys a smaller company only to hire the entire team without doing a complete end run around the investors. When a startup gets acquihired, shareholders are likely to get back just pennies for every dollar they invested, while a B- or C-level banker in a bad suit gets paid a $50,000 retainer and $100,000 minimum commission to sell that company for $500,000 to $2 million.

It's ugly and it sucks and no one wins except maybe the acquirer, who gains a dozen talented new employees for far less than the cost they would have paid headhunters to recruit those individuals and without losing all of the time it would have taken them to learn how to work together. As a bonus, there's always a chance that the product they were working on becomes meaningful.

LITTLE BIRDS AND BIG VULTURES

In the recent fire sale of a promising startup called Little Bird, a hired CEO had run the company into the ground, turning $1 million in sales in the year he joined into $750,000 the next year. He then hired a banker to sell the company that he destroyed.

When the final sale price of around $400,000 was presented to me for my signature, I learned that almost 40 percent of that was going to the banker and the CEO's severance package and that the CEO had sent some employees to the acquiring company in advance of the deal without the consent of the investors—which sounds legally actionable to me, but taking legal action against startups you've invested in is often a waste of time, as I explained in chapter 9.

To get eight cents on the dollar going to investors with a company making $750,000 a year and being bought for way less than one times revenue was bizarre.

Of course, there is little you can do in these situations, as you're usually fighting with a bunch of vultures over a festering corpse. I withheld my signature until I extracted $100,000 in advisor shares in the acquiring company that were very tightly bound to me, my LPs (limited partners), and my syndicate.

The failed CEO kept telling me that I was holding up the sale. I kept telling him he ran the company into the ground, so it was shameful of him to collect a huge severance on the way out. Hired CEOs almost never work out, and the ones who care more about their severance packages than the business succeeding in its mission—like this one—are the worst of a bad breed.

He said I would ruin the deal if I talked to the acquiring CEO, but I did it anyway. The CEO, it turns out, was a fan of my podcast and my magazine, *Silicon Alley Reporter,* from the '90s. He was happy to have me on his board of advisors.

So, there is a chance that an eight-cents-on-the-dollar deal that was being rammed down my throat might still wind up breaking even or returning two times my investment or more. For me, that's glorious because all returns have value—no matter if they're ten or twenty or fifty cents on the dollar. If I get two times my money back on this deal, it will be another $200,000 I can deploy into eight other startups—and that is why I fight and never give up.

I was a money-losing poker player for the first four years because I would leave when I lost a certain amount of money. Today I'm a cash-positive poker player because I try to leave the table only after I've won a big pot, buying in over and over again until I do.

SMART AND GETS THINGS DONE

Other M&A situations come from out of the blue and you're dragged along. My friend Joel Spolsky, a fantastic founder in New York City, invited me to invest in his Trello task management software after guest starring on my podcast. I tossed in $100,000 and two years after I did, I got an email alert that a public company had purchased Trello, providing us with a return of more than eight times.

Yum! Yum! for JCal!

In these situations, you receive a bunch of paperwork to sign and you are "dragged along" with the majority of the shareholders. You don't have a choice, as your agreement states that if the majority decides to sell, then the company is sold. As an angel, you sometimes have very little control, but you have many swings at bat.

You sign the paperwork and collect your return and go back to the plate and start swinging the bat again. Singles and doubles aren't home runs, but they frequently win the game. Some angels never hit a hundred-times return, but they are so good at getting five and ten times their money on deals that it adds up.

EVERYBODY WANTS YOU

"Great companies are bought, not sold" is a timeless adage here in Silicon Valley. The best possible situation you can be in is to have a growing company with a huge pile of cash and massive interest from big companies looking to acquire you.

The only thing better than this is when there is absolute fear and paranoia among your potential acquirers that one of those other companies is going to snap yours up before they do.

That's exactly what happened with Instagram and WhatsApp, both of which were acquired by Mark Zuckerberg. I say they were acquired by Zuckerberg for a reason: he did these deals personally and reportedly without needing to get permission from his board. The unique corporate structure at Facebook, as well as Zuckerberg's persuasiveness and aggressive pursuit of Google's advertising market share, have made him the best acquirer in the business since, well, Google.

Instagram had a long-standing relationship with Twitter, and it felt like a no-brainer that Kevin Systrom would sell to the then-booming social network. Instagram was doing so well that it raised $50 million in 2012 less than a week before selling the business to Facebook for $1 billion.

Instagram investors got a massive and quick return, but, much like YouTube investors, they were left wondering what could have been. If Instagram was an independent company today, with its monthly active users number comparable to Twitter's, it would easily be worth more than $10 billion.

Instagram sold way too early, which is of course a high-class problem. We don't know if the Instagram shareholders kept their Facebook stock as it doubled over and over again or if they sold it. And we don't know if Instagram could have monetized their audience, grown their infrastructure, or iterated on their product as well as they have as part of Facebook.

Either way, Instagram was a critical piece in Facebook's ascension and the Google and Twitter folks were not happy about the sale.

Google was an M&A grandmaster for the better part of a decade, with most of their success outside of their search engine and Gmail coming from writing checks. They bought their mobile operating system Android in 2005, YouTube in 2006, DoubleClick in 2007, and the pay-per-click contextual ad platform Applied Semantics in 2003.

However, when a company gets huge and the founders are ten times ahead of the next closest competitor, as Google was with Facebook, you can get lazy. While Google was busy building self-driving cars and high-speed internet balloons, Zuckerberg grabbed hundreds of millions of unique users that were obsessed with Instagram and WhatsApp, and he now has almost two billion monthly users around the globe.

The WhatsApp acquisition was spectacular, coming in at $19 billion. Unknown to me, I was an LP in one of the funds that backed WhatsApp and I got a huge check for being in that fund. Facebook looked crazy for buying WhatsApp for more than 10 percent of their market cap at the time, but what if Google had gotten it? Or Apple? Or Microsoft?

WhatsApp was a social network based on your phone book, which was really the only thing that could potentially derail Facebook, so they had to buy it. Risking 10 percent of your equity is better than losing 50 percent of it.

Operators wanting to buy your startup is the second-most-positive sign in all of entrepreneurship. The only sign that's better is paying customers raving to their friends about how awesome your product is.

When you approach twenty-five companies about buying your startup and not a single one of them gives you a term sheet, you have figured out, frankly, that you and your business suck—at least right now.

Get back to work. You're blowing it!

CHAPTER 31

FINDING YOUR GROOVE

WHAT'S YOUR STRATEGY?

"Successful startups have a hundred angels but failures are orphans."

Or something like that.

There are dozens of theories about why startups succeed, from "It's all about timing" to "You're investing in founders" to "It's the market that makes the startup."

It's essential for us humans to build unifying theories for complex and random systems because we're scared little bugs counting the days before our death while sitting on a random rock orbiting one of a trillion suns in a random universe that we know so little about.

We create frameworks for everything from the meaning of life

("It's all a big nothing."—Livia Soprano), consciousness (we're living in a simulation), making great movies (conflict, character, acting, or dialogue), and being great parents (model the behavior you want to see in your kids), so it's no wonder we put so much effort into figuring out why *these* two people with an idea change the world from their garage, but *those* two people in an identical garage a few blocks over change nothing but their LinkedIn profiles.

Many of these theories we create are the products of the cognitive biases humans unknowingly suffer from, including "confirmation bias," where the person holding a belief searches out and remembers things that back up that very belief (efficient!), to the "negativity bias," which states that bad shit sticks with us and impacts our future decisions more than good shit.

For example, if you lost your money investing in a web-based photo sharing service, you might quickly dismiss the unicorn Instagram because of your "negative bias" for the photo space, never realizing that the "why now?" (see chapter 18) of photo filters combined with high-resolution cameras on mobile phones with powerful processors has the potential to turn everyone on the planet into a professional photographer.

Instagram exploded because it let everyone create sepia tones and blurred depth of field photos without spending $5,000 on a huge camera, expensive lenses, flash cards, and readers, all while wasting hours in Photoshop—which also cost hundreds of dollars!

It was a miracle that we now take for granted.

Let that sink in for a moment, because in almost every investment decision you'll face, some of your bias will be unknowingly triggered.

Remember, we have more blind spots than we do clear vision, so you must unlearn what you have learned to be a successful angel.

SOME ANGELS BET ON FOUNDERS

I always tell folks that I don't need to figure out if your product will succeed, I just need to know if you will succeed. If I have a gift in this angel investing game, it's that I'm good at reading people and figuring out how meaningful winning will be to them.

It probably comes from years of trying to read the best poker players in the world—and failing often.

Some of the techniques deployed in poker are applicable to startups, including "putting people on a range of hands." What this means in poker is that after playing with a person for a couple of hours, you should be able to narrow down what two cards they have by their poker actions (betting, raising, going all in) and by their non-poker-related behaviors (playing with their chips, leaning forward or backward, talking more or less than they normally do, drinking water, etc.).

This is a bit of art and a bit of science in poker, because the people who are very good at the game actually know what the common tells are and will "level you" by throwing out tells that historically equal weakness (i.e., talking a bunch and leaning in over their chips) when they're really strong, while acting strong when they're weak (leaning back and being quiet is the classic tell for strength. For example, picture a guy from Texas with a big hat leaning back and chomping on a cigar with a look on his face that says, "Go ahead, call my bet so I can flip over my cards and break your heart").

In the startup game, we generally don't have this kind of "leveling," but there is plenty of gamesmanship.

For example, the founder of Theranos, Elizabeth Holmes, took to wearing black turtlenecks like Steve Jobs and she dropped out of college just like Bill Gates and Mark Zuckerberg. She claimed she could do blood tests with micro samples of blood taken from a pinprick as opposed to drawing vial after vial of blood from your arm.

A few savvy investors passed when Holmes wouldn't show them the technology, as they should have. They didn't buy into her act. She claimed trade secrets when they asked to look at the tech, which was an obvious—but perhaps unconscious—bid to imitate Steve Jobs. Famously, Jobs deployed all kinds of secret labs, iron-clad nondisclosure agreements (NDAs), and security procedures to create an aura of importance around the next mouse or iMac.

But many equally smart investors fell for Holmes's story and they are now doing something you never see in Silicon Valley: they are suing their own portfolio company. Suing a startup you invest in is extremely rare because it's a very hard case to win.

Think about it: everyone who invests in startups for a living has a long list of failures that prove they know how risky this all is. All the documents we sign, all the interviews we give at conferences, and all of the industry statistics show a clear expectation that you will lose your money on most and make your returns on a few—perhaps just one—investment.

What judge or jury is going to believe that a professional investor didn't understand the risks in investing in a college dropout who had never run a business, and who claimed she had a secret technology that none of the other major blood testing companies could figure out over decades of research, that could diagnose diseases with a pinprick of blood?

Even the OJ jury, after doing tequila shots for hours in the hot sun, wouldn't side with the investors—unless they were presented with massive undeniable fraud.

So, the only motivation a reasonable investor would have to sue a startup they invested in is if they felt they were intentionally duped. This is why due diligence is important (see chapter 24), especially in later stages when there is actual data that can be verified. Remember, however, that in the case of Theranos, Holmes used the "tell" of Steve Jobs–like secrecy as a way to avoid showing investors the technology.

And, apparently, some of them fell for it and invested without seeing the technology.

How would an investor have been able to avoid backing Holmes, who at this point is facing assault from all sides, including the government, former employees, and investors?

Fairly simple: insist on seeing the technology early on with someone who has worked in the blood-testing space and who had signed an NDA with Theranos. It's a perfectly reasonable request.

If Theranos says no, you have an easy out because who wants to be involved with a founder with no track record and who doesn't trust you enough to let you see what you're investing in? That's like a director who has never made a film telling a money producer, "No, I can't show you the script of this movie even though you're funding it."

What?!

Now, after the Theranos product was released for a small set of diseases, there was an even simpler way to vet it: go to a random store offering the Theranos tests and take them and compare the results to traditional blood tests.

Ironically, that's exactly what a former Apple executive, Jean-Louis Gassée, who worked for Steve Jobs, did.

His results showed that the Theranos tests didn't work and Holmes never responded.

So, back to poker for a moment. I could go into a ton of examples of poker hands here, but the easiest one that even people who don't play poker could understand is the following.

Imagine you're playing poker with someone who hasn't played any hands in the past three hours. This person would be considered a "tight" player because they only play the best hands (say two aces or two kings, or an ace and king). They get to bet first, before you do, and they put out a raise. You re-raise them and they quickly call. Do you think they are playing a 5 and an 8, or do you think they have a big pocket pair, like two aces, kings, queens, jacks, or 10s?

Did they really wait hours and hours to play a shitty hand like a 5 and an 8?

If after the next set of cards comes out (the flop) and it's ace, 6, 7, and they bet again, now what do you think they have? Did they wait hours and hours at the hopes of having 5, 6, 7, and 8 so they could draw to a straight (by getting a 4 or 9)? Of course not.

Most folks in poker are easy to read. They play what is called ABC poker, which is to say, they do what is expected. It's only the top 20 percent that are the challenge.

Elizabeth Holmes represents that top 20 percent of sophisticated, and often pathologically deranged, startup founders who will do anything it takes to win, from playing a part to outright lying to investors.

At the time of publishing this book, Theranos was spinning around the drain of the toilet (end of metaphor, I think you get it). Perhaps by the time you read this she will have magically produced her technology after ten-plus years in development and filibustering when asked to show it—or maybe she'll be in jail and become the tech version of Bernie Madoff.

Anything is possible, but I think we all know what's probable in this case.

Either way, Jennifer Lawrence is set to play her in the movie by Adam McKay, the director of *The Big Short*. I'm hoping to get a cameo as an angel who laughs and passes on investing when she tells me I can't see the technology.

It could happen.

On the other side of the "people theory of startups" are founders who have a singular focus and execute at the highest level. Zuckerberg comes to mind not for being a visionary but for having a superhuman level of focus—like the Terminator.

Zuck was able to see what Friendster and MySpace created in social media and execute, in the early days, about 20 percent to 50 percent better than they did on any individual feature. Facebook's site was notably faster and its design was easier to understand.

Then he made the sign-up flow 50 percent better by not letting you see profiles before you signed up and the entire service 100 percent better by building a better newsfeed—inspired by Twitter's work.

After that, he sorted the newsfeed 50 percent better than Twitter's by sorting not chronologically but by which posts got the most likes and comments (i.e., engagement). That's why, when you load Twitter, you see a bunch of random tweets from the past fifteen minutes, but when you open Facebook you're greeted with a baby announcement, a death announcement, and the most popular viral video in the system with a note about which of your friends really like watching chubby pandas rolling around in the mud. (FYI, it's all of them. I just saved you a click.)

Important to note that Zuck and Holmes both dropped out of school.

Important to note that Zuck and Holmes both wear the same simple "uniform" every day (Zuck wears a hoodie and gray T-shirt, she the Jobs black turtleneck).

Important to note that Zuck and Holmes both believed they were building the most important company in the world.

However, Zuck showed his work and explained what they were doing and why to investors and the press. It was very clear after a couple of years of consistent product cycles that there were few people who could hold their focus on incremental product improvement and growth the way Zuck had.

Zuck might not be the most creative founder we've seen, but he is certainly the most consistent and terrifying. Just like Arnold Schwarzenegger's Terminator, everyone knows that Zuck will not stop.

SOME ANGELS WANT TO SOLVE A PROBLEM

"What problem do you solve?" is a classic venture capitalist question that is sometimes phrased as "Is your startup a vitamin or a painkiller?" or "What pain do you remove?"

The bottom line is that many of the great companies in the world were built on the promise of removing pain from people's lives. Sometimes folks have a huge problem and they are searching for a solution.

When I started working in Manhattan in the late 1980s, all of the law firms still had huge mailrooms with large staffs of messengers, who would race around Manhattan with bundles of documents. It was always an interesting place for me, as a person who was building computer networks for law firms, to visit because I knew it would soon be gone.

My first jobs were setting up what was called "document management" systems on LANs (local area networks).

When we visited a law firm and studied how they went from a contract to signed contract, it went something like this: a lawyer would draft a document on paper or dictate it to their secretary who would send it to the "typing pool," which was a room full of, you guessed it, people on typewriters creating documents.

The final draft would get proofed and sent to the "copy room," which was a room full of photocopy machines, before going to the mailroom to be sent by cannabis-powered messengers whipping through Manhattan on ten-speed bikes, whose frames were tightly wrapped in electrical tape to disguise their value and protect them.

The signed copies, as well as all the revisions, would come

back and be sent to the document storage lockers in the basement and a warehouse in Queens.

The document management software and email systems we were installing solved so many of these problems that law firms would literally spend thousands of dollars per year per attorney installing and maintaining them.

Lawyers couldn't spend their money fast enough with LAN Systems, the company I worked for.

We held parties, had a bonus program, took Lincoln Town Cars home every night, and our bosses took us to Scores, a strip club, every month with our clients, buying thousands of dollars' worth of "funny money," to spend on strippers.

We solved many pain points and were paid handsomely to do so. We eliminated the typing pool; we eliminated half the secretaries taking dictation because lawyers started cutting and pasting documents. We made the lawyers bionic by making templates for common documents where they filled in the blanks.

I could always tell how important our solution was because the top partners in a firm would come to the meetings with us and go over every single aspect of the software and network and what it could do. Can two of us work on the same document at a time? Can my partner in Los Angeles edit this same document or do I need to FedEx them a floppy disk?

All day long they dealt with pain, and the power of the networks and software eliminated their headaches so deftly that they created budgets for IT staffs that ballooned to over 10 percent of their total staff.

When you look at a startup that is creating the eighty-ninth photo sharing app, you have to ask yourself, Is this really solving any major pain points?

I like to put pain points into two buckets: Indiana Jones and Louis C.K.

If you remember the second Indiana Jones movie, with the greatest opening of any movie ever, Indy is trading a relic with some gangsters, who upon consummating the deal by spinning a huge diamond in exchange for an urn filled with ashes on a lazy Susan, inform Indiana Jones that he just drank poison in his champagne and that they have the only antidote and he must spin the diamond back to them to get the antidote.

Put aside the massive gaps in logic in this scenario and think about the problem of having just drunk poison and someone having the antidote.

That's as powerful as it gets, and that's why rattlesnake venom is expensive and pharmaceutical companies are so hated because they can charge so much for lifesaving drugs.

Most startups do not cure death, but if you've found one that does, put down this book and email me immediately at jason@ calacanis.com.

Of course, some startups are working on problems that in the long term will lower the numbers of death, but they are less critical than those in the Indiana Jones example. They include Uber and Tesla creating self-driving car technology that will reduce the number of deaths on the road here in the United States from thirty thousand–plus a year to thirty a year in the next thirty years, I predict.

Reducing death in short-and long-term situations is virtuous, but there are more pragmatic things startups work on, like the ability to show you the various versions of a document you've worked on, or collaborate on that document over thousands of miles in real time.

Microsoft has had two major cash cows over the years, Windows and Microsoft Office. The latter included Word and Excel, which made billions of dollars in profits by solving these very real pain points I've mentioned.

Of course, Office created a new set of pain points, the most notable of which was that the local storage of documents on fragile hard drives that frequently failed or were corrupted by viruses resulted in the loss of many manuscripts and business plans. These pain points created huge new categories of startups, including external hard drives, antivirus software, and backup software.

Eventually, when bandwidth and server storage costs plummeted, Dropbox pioneered a solution that solved the very real problem of lost documents: the cloud.

In ten short years, Dropbox and competitor Box, along with Amazon Web Services (AWS), have generated tens of billions of dollars in value for investors, while removing a massive pain point for consumers (lost documents).

Now the cloud has brought forth a new series of problems that will inspire a new cluster of startups to solve. The two biggest problems the cloud has brought forth seem to be, so far, the security of data stored in the cloud, which is resulting in trade secrets being stolen and ransom being charged to those who don't have two-factor authentication turned on.

The second problem that has emerged is searching and sorting through the massive amount of data being thrown into the cloud.

However, do you think either of these problems is as dire as the ones that have come before them? Are they removing as much pain—probably not. The problems around documents have been worked on for more than half a century by technology companies, so many of the problems are now becoming softer and more infrequent.

Which leads to the hilarious Louis C.K. bit on Conan O'Brien's show, in which he explained how "everything is amazing right now and nobody's happy." Louis chronicles how people used to deal with things like getting money from a bank (going inside and waiting in line) before explaining how early credit cards used to work.

For those of you who were born after 1990, it went something like this: you gave your card to a waiter, who used a pen to fill out a carbon copy form with your name and number, before sliding it in a medieval machine that made an impression of your card on the paper (this could take three or four back-and-forth motions), and then calling the credit card company to talk to a human operator who would give the waiter an authorization code.

This process could take more than ten minutes. I know because I used to do it at my dad's bar in the '80s.

Of course, all those carbon copies had to be split apart and mailed to the credit card company, which would send the money to the bar and a paper statement to the individual over postal mail. You the consumer would take out your checkbook and write a check and put it in an envelope and mail it to the credit card company.

Today you tap your card or phone and get your receipt in your email box and the money is typically deducted from your bank account—all before you get up to leave the dinner table.

In another ten years, you will look into a retina scanner at checkout and carry no money or credit cards. Amazon has already demonstrated this with their checkout-free grocery stores.

Louis C.K. ends his bit with how entitled people are when flying, explaining how pissed off his seatmate was when the internet on his flight went down.

In-flight internet is the perfect example of a soft problem that people thought was hard. Sure, people said they would pay for Wi-Fi on flights, and hundreds of millions of dollars were invested in in-flight internet companies, but the truth is that consumers lied.

Consumers were over the moon with the concept of internet access on flight and they said they would pay for it. Investors and founders were excited, too, but when presented with the option of spending about $5 an hour for internet access, people didn't bite.

The truth was, being without the internet for one to five hours wasn't a hard problem for people—it was a nice respite. Plus, people quickly learned to download games, movies, books, podcasts, music playlists, and audiobooks to their devices before they left for the airport and while on their unlimited home broadband internet connections.

In-flight internet shows a confirmation bias in investors and founders, because they focused on the data that pointed to mass adoption (surveys, mobile data subscribers, dial-up subscribers, the cost vs. in-flight movies and their ticket) while ignoring the obvious: people have said for ages that they love to read, sleep, and watch movies on flights—none of which require internet.

Just like phones on planes, which used to be on the back of

every headrest, the pain wasn't deep and often, like it needs to be for people to pay.

Make an *x* axis and *y* axis and name them "intensity of pain" and "frequency of people experiencing that pain." In the top right, you have things that are very painful and that you experience all the time; in the bottom left you have things that are not painful and that don't happen that often. Then there are things that are very painful and infrequent or not very painful but very frequent.

You can put the pain of not having internet in the bottom left, even though we act like it's in the top right.

Now, some products exist to delight their customers, like Disneyland, ice cream, and the movies, and they make serious bank without taking away any pain.

You've probably never said "I'm in serious pain right now because I'm not waiting in line to go on a roller coaster" or "I've got to figure out a way to put some cold, fat, and sugar in my mouth quickly!"

The only time I can remember being physically in pain wanting to see a movie was *The Empire Strikes Back*, so much so that I left school at noon, cut three classes, and was first in line at the Fortway Theatre in Brooklyn. My father got a call from my junior high school and drove directly to the movie theater, knowing I would be there.

I thought he was going to take a swing at me when he pulled up and motioned for me to come to him. I braced for impact, because I'd taken a shot or two from him before, and was delighted to see him pull $40 from his pocket and say, "Get tickets for your brothers, too, and don't cut school again."

Dealing with my dad was always a mixture of delight and pain, but I'll save all of that for another book.

SOME ANGELS BET ON DELIGHT

As I mentioned, some startups are so delightful to use that people can't live without them and will pay a premium for them. These startups have pricing power, and pricing power is a magical thing in the world of business because it's rare and because it results in obscene returns.

Delight startups are the opposite of problem startups. It's common to hear investors ask, "Is your startup a vitamin or a painkiller?"

Apple makes products that are so aesthetically delightful, even when years behind competitors' products, that they command a massive premium. An Android phone with better hardware specs and better features will still sell for hundreds of dollars less than an iPhone. Same with a laptop or headphones from anyone who isn't Apple.

Most of all, we saw this when Apple launched their Cinema Display, which came in a gorgeous brushed aluminum casing, but at twice the price as the same-quality monitor from Dell. Apple fanboys and-girls bought the monitor with the sexy logo for upward of $1,000 more. Insane!

There is a simple tool for figuring out how delightful a startup's product is. It's called NPS and it stands for Net Promoter Score. You've probably taken an NPS survey before. An NPS measures the willingness of customers to recommend a company's products or services to others. Smart founders use the feedback from NPS surveys to improve their services and maximize their growth.

SOME ANGELS BET ON MARKETS

There are some investors who feel it's the market that makes the startup. They will look at the size of the insurance, food, or transportation industries and say, "Technology is going to massively impact these industries—let's find startups who are innovating in this market."

If you thought the food market was ripe for disruption, you might look at the massive trend of people wanting to eat more protein—especially red meat—and try to find mock hamburger companies or people who think they will be able to 3-D print a steak. You might consider alternative proteins, like a startup I've considered investing in that is focused on cricket protein flour (the cookies taste awesome).

Other folks will look at the transportation space and see that cars are unused 95 percent of the time and conclude that car ownership will end and car sharing will be the future. They might think Uber or Zipcar will be the big winners in this space, but as you can see from the performance of those two companies, they are two very different concepts. In the first solution, you are driven door to door, but in the second you take possession of a car for a short period and drive—and park—yourself.

The latter is a closer analogy to what people do with car ownership, so that might seem like the easier solution for people to embrace, but it's turned out to be the opposite—people don't just want to give up car ownership, they never want to even be in possession of one!

This is why the market strategy is not as effective as the founder and problem theories of startups, in my mind.

The good news is you don't need to pick one theory and live by it. You can be holistic and run a startup through all of these theories and see where they wind up. Then convince yourself to ignore the ones you don't like and use your gut!

CHAPTER 32

WHERE DOES YOUR ANGEL STORY END?

Writing this book has been one of the most reflective and rewarding processes of my life. I'm glad I told my literary agent and rabbi, John Brockman, that I wanted to wait until I had "one more big win" to write a book because, as I codify my playbook, I'm asking myself if I still want to keep running it.

That's why you don't see any books on angel investing or meet many career angel investors. In fact, there have only been a handful of people who have done angel investing for a complete decade and I am on a first-name basis with all of them: Esther Dyson, Mark Cuban, Stewart Alsop, Mitch Kapor, and Ron Conway top my list of angels who just won't stop.

Angel investing, as we've learned, is a unique vocation, because if you're qualified to be an angel, you are overqualified to be a venture capitalist, and venture capitalists have a much easier and more financially rewarding life.

Angels deal with a mortality rate in the 80 and 90 percent range, which can make your life feel more like that of a hospice worker than a financial wizard. Venture capitalists can move so far upstream that they deal with a mortality rate half that—or less—of an angel.

Oh yeah, because venture capitalists are putting more money into a smaller number of deals, they have fewer people calling them and fewer deals to negotiate. As a reward for doing less than angel investors, they get paid more by placing a small number of bigger bets and have the management fee teat to suckle on.

These management fees are an advance on returns paid to venture capitalists by LPs every year to cover their salaries and overhead. It's typically 2 to 3 percent of the total amount raised—every single year.

I've been asked to join a number of venture firms over the years, which would allow me to make more money and have no overhead. The only requirements would be that I engage in one or two new investments a year and be on the boards of six or eight startups. I could take off summers and winters, too, and jet off to Italy and Aspen and . . . and . . . Fuck, I should do that!

Why don't I? Well, to be honest, as much as I love being an angel, I'm tempted. Seriously tempted. Why not spend more time with my kids and less time hustling? Why not wait under the basket for the next Jason Calacanis to bring the ball all the way down the court before I slam-dunk it and get the max money deal for scoring the most points on the team?

That's the biggest danger for angels: success. If you hit a huge win, you're going to quit, almost everyone does, because the chances of me hitting another Uber is next to impossible (they come once a decade), and while the chances of me hitting another Thumbtack is almost assured, the billion-dollar exits are never going to be the same level as the $50 billion or $100 billion or $250 billion ones.

But back to you. Here are all the common scenarios of what will happen if you invest in thirty startups in the manner I've described in this book, with the first ten being $1,000 syndicates and the next twenty being $25,000 bets, and then putting an extra $100,000 into each of the top five startups in your portfolio.

In this scenario, you will have put $510,000 into your first thirty deals, watched for winners, and put another $500,000 into the winners. You'll have put just over $1 million to work.

YOU RETURN LESS THAN YOU INVESTED

If 90 percent of your startups die and five have modest exits that return just your money invested, you will have gotten back around $500,000 of your $1 million, losing a half-million dollars. As a high-net-worth individual, this loss will not feel great, but you will have only lost 5 to 10 percent of your $5 million to $10 million net worth. You're rich and your other investments returning 5 percent a year in the stock market will easily make up for this $500,000 loss.

You'll be able to study your investment thesis and either use the exact same exit strategy in your next thirty startups or upgrade your strategy and do even better. Certainly, you've learned something from your three to five years of angel investing that will give you an edge when you do the next thirty investments.

If you're exhausted from angel investing but you are addicted to startups, you'll have a nice track record with founders that will allow you to join a venture capital firm with a $500,000 starting salary, making this a fantastic investment similar to getting your undergrad and graduate degrees!

YOU RETURN WHAT YOU INVESTED

Many angels get a push, which means you learned a hell of a lot and came out even, building your network and knowledge on the house. Sort of like going to Vegas for a long weekend, getting comped for your room and some fancy meals because you spend hours having a blast playing craps or blackjack. The trip was free and your account is whole.

You now have the option to keep being an angel, join a firm, or perhaps even take a management team or board seat at your highest-performing investment, getting you 1 to 2 percent of the company and a nice salary as you help build the company to a billion.

This happens often in the angel and venture community, with investors getting bored placing bets and wanting to be in the game. With the insider experience you got working with your top-performing company, you're going to be able to negotiate a great deal with new founders who respect you for betting on them early, and together you'll get to an amazing outcome.

YOU RETURN TWO TO FIVE TIMES WHAT YOU INVESTED

If you put $1 million to work in this scenario of investing for a year, you could return $2 million to $5 million by simply having your top five double down bets (those where you put an extra $100,000 on top of your first bet of $1,000 or $25,000) return four to ten times each, or even one of them returning fifty times your investment. While a fifty-times return isn't common, four- to ten-times returns happen all the time in Silicon Valley (remember, you want to invest in Silicon Valley, where you get the ace of spades as your first card every time; see chapter 6).

If this happens, you will not only have the ability to join one of your startups, get on boards, or join a venture capital firm, but you will also have a track record to raise your own fund by sharing your return data with all the other rich people you've met, giving you a large multiplier on your future investing. Raising your own fund is another book, and since I've only raised one small $10 million fund, I'm not the person to write that book—yet.

YOU RETURN MORE THAN FIVE TO ONE HUNDRED TIMES WHAT YOU INVESTED

Congratulations. In all likelihood, one of your bets went supernova and you got two hundred or three hundred or four hundred times your money. A company you invested in at a $4 million valuation got sold or went public for $5 billion or

$10 billion and you now have $25 million to $100 million in returns.

The F-U money will last a lifetime and your kids are going to have to deal with their trust funds and free ride in college, not to mention the shadow their rich angel-investing mom (or dad) has cast upon them—provided you don't get divorced, get addicted to flying private, or buy a boat.

Soak in what you've learned by hitting a home run in your first thirty bets while appreciating the randomness of life. You didn't exactly hit the lottery, but you did get lucky because your thirty bets probably weren't all that different from the bets of people who lost money or broke even. In fact, almost all angels probably have a very similar return profile if you take out their top investment—and the exact same return profile if you take out their top three hits.

If you hit a home run like this, you are a legend in our industry and can work for a top-tier firm or even start your own incubator like I did, with investors and founders flocking to it, assuming that you have the Midas touch—even if we both know no one actually does.

Life is random, but luck isn't.

Lucky people surround themselves with the most successful people in the world and take chances. It isn't hard or impossible. It just takes work.

Do the work.

Trust me, just do the work.

ACKNOWLEDGMENTS

Thanks to my agent, John Brockman, for including me in everything he does and for patiently counseling me on my career, life, and writing. Max Brockman and the team at Brockman Inc. have been spectacularly professional and supportive during this process—I feel so blessed to be on the team.

Thanks to Brian Alvey, who coached me through this book over nineteen very full days. He organized the manuscript diligently while telling me candidly when I had jumped the fence and needed to rein it in. More important, Brian has been a friend to me for three decades, from Bay Ridge to the Bay Area. I'm looking forward to the next three decades.

Thanks to my brilliant, lovely, and supportive wife, Jade, who took care of our identical twin daughters, two bulldogs, and our seven-year-old, London, all while moving into our new home and allowing me to stay in the zone while I "banged out a few more pages."

My two brothers, Jamie and Josh, who have always looked out for me—one for all and all for one. I mentioned my mom in the dedication, but it's worth stating again that she taught me how to work hard and stay humble—and to not drop so many f-bombs.

Special thanks to team members past and present, who have worked by my side to support founders and inspire innovation, including—but not limited to—Tyler "Insights From" Crowley, Lon Harris, Jason Krute, Brice Milano, Ashley Whitehurst, Luke Lightning, Jason Demant, Emmy Award–winning producer Jacqui Deegan, and Elliot Cook.

To mentors and friends, too many to count, including Roelof Botha, who pushed me to start investing; David Sacks and Naval Ravikant, who told me to start a fund; and Fred Wilson, who bought the first ad in *Silicon Alley Reporter*. To Bill Lee, who told everyone to back me; Chamath Palihapitiya, who always has time for a "walk and talk"; and David Goldberg, whose wise take always helped keep me centered.

And most of all, to all the founders who allowed me to join them on their journey—especially Travis Kalanick and Garrett Camp of Uber, who have made me look much smarter than I'll ever be.

They say no one gets there alone, and halfway through my career, I can tell you this is the truest things I know.

Jason Calacanis
Calacanis.com

ABOUT THE AUTHOR

JASON CALACANIS is a technology entrepreneur, angel investor, and the host of the popular weekly podcast *This Week in Startups.* The founder of a series of conferences that bring entrepreneurs together with potential investors, he was a "scout" for top-tier Silicon Valley venture capital firm Sequoia Capital and frequently appears in the media. He lives in San Francisco, California.